40
Questions
to Change
Your Life

40
Questions
to Change
Your Life

John Mason

SPIRE

© 2018 by John Mason

Published by Revell
a division of Baker Publishing Group
PO Box 6287, Grand Rapids, MI 49516-6287
www.revellbooks.com

Spire edition published 2021
ISBN 978-0-8007-4011-5
eISBN 978-1-4934-3173-1

Previously published in 2018 under the title *Seize Today*

Printed in the United States of America

22   23   24   25   26   27   7   6   5   4   3   2

I am proud to dedicate this book to my beautiful wife, Linda; our four great kids, Michelle, Greg, Mike, and Dave; my two daughters-in-law, Brittany and Kelley; and my three grandchildren, Emma, Olivia, and Beckett.

To Linda, for your prayers and love.

To Michelle, for your dedication and unwavering commitment to excellence.

To Greg, for your peaceful faith and support.

To Mike, for your creativity and worshipful heart.

To Dave, for your competitive spirit and "Dave and Dad" fun.

To my dear mom, who has always loved me unconditionally. The best mom in the world!

To Brittany and Kelley, for your love for my sons and your love for the Lord.

To Emma, Olivia, and Beckett, for the sweetness, laughter, and abundance of love you've brought to our entire family.

Your support, help, encouragement, sense of humor, and prayers sustain and bless me every day.

Contents

Acknowledgments

I'd like to thank Lonnie Hull DuPont for her excellent thoughts on how to make this book better. Her candor, humor, and expertise are always appreciated.

Introduction

We've all heard the expression *carpe diem*, "seize the day." It's a great thought and one I embrace. In this book, *40 Questions to Change Your Life*, I hope to take that idea one step further for you.

When you seize the day, how do you know what to do, what to choose, or where to go? I believe the answer is best found by asking the right questions.

In this book, I present forty key questions and teachings I know will unlock answers for your life. The Bible statements "You have not because you ask not" (James 4:2 ABPE) and "Ask and you will receive" (John 16:24 NIV) are as true today as they were two thousand years ago.

It's been said you can judge a man by his questions as much as by his answers. I believe you're where you are today because of the questions you've asked.

To get where you want to be, you must ask the right questions. The difference between people who are successful and those who aren't is that successful people ask better questions and therefore get better results.

13

Do you ask enough questions, or do you settle for what you know? What are the questions that are shaping *your* life?

Seize your way, every day. Every person is created equal in this regard; we're all given twenty-four hours each day. You'll find that the secret to your success is hidden in your daily routine. What we all do each day matters. So seize today by asking the right questions.

Question 1

When was the last time you astonished yourself?

I obtained an amazing job a few years after graduating from college. It all began when I received a phone call out of the blue. I was enrolled full-time in an MBA program, but this was too good to pass up.

The job opportunity was beyond my wildest imagination: assistant to the chairman of the board of the largest bank in Oklahoma. I'll never forget going through seven interviews, starting in human resources all the way through the chairman and president, and finally receiving a job offer at only twenty-four years of age. And I was about to get an invaluable perspective from the top down.

As I worked directly for the chairman of the board, my responsibilities included serving on many boards for the bank, giving speeches for the president and chairman, teaching other top executives how to communicate to an audience, sitting in on board meetings, overseeing the executive dining room floor, and running the bank's tennis tournament (which included Jimmy Connors, Stan Smith, Roscoe Tanner, and many other of the world's top players). I didn't fully realize it at the time, but my view of business and leadership would never be the same.

I thought I was thinking "big" before this job, but there was a much bigger world out there. That's true for you too.

Life is too short to think small. Rather, do as Joel Budd encourages us to: "March off the map." Most people could do more than they think they can, but they usually do less than they think they can. You never know what you cannot do until you try.

I agree in principle with Oscar Wilde when he said, "Moderation is a fatal thing. Nothing succeeds like excess." Charles Schwab said, "When a man has put a limit on what he will do, he has put a limit on what he can do."

The answer to your future lies outside the confines of where you are today. I like to say that if you want to see if you can really swim, don't frustrate yourself with shallow water. Launch out into the deep. Get out of the shallow end of the pool of life.

Any person who selects a goal in life that can be fully achieved without God's help has defined their own limitations. Rather, as Art Sepulveda says, "Be a history maker and a world shaker."

Go where you have never gone before. Determine to see and do amazing things you've never imagined. You will find that great leaders are rarely "realistic" by other people's standards.

Dr. J. A. Holmes said, "Never tell a young person that something cannot be done. God may have been waiting for centuries for somebody ignorant enough of the impossible to do that thing." If *you* devalue your dreams, rest assured no one else will raise the price.

Ronald McNair said, "You only become a winner if you are willing to walk over the edge." The Bible tells us, "The things which are impossible with men are possible with God" (Luke 18:27).

When you climb the tallest tree, you can see farther than you imagined when on the ground. Gloria Swanson said, "Never say never. Never is a long, undependable thing, and life is too full of rich possibilities to have restrictions placed upon it."

To believe an idea impossible is to make it so. Consider how many fantastic projects have died because of small thinking or have been strangled in their birth by a cowardly imagination. I like what Comte de Mirabeau said. When he heard the word *impossible*, he responded, "Never let me hear that foolish word again."

Somebody is always doing what somebody else said couldn't be done. Dare to think unthinkable thoughts. Pearl Buck said, "All things are possible until they are proved impossible—and even the impossible may only be so, as of now." John Ruskin said, "Dream lofty dreams, and as you dream, so you shall become. Your vision is the promise of what you shall at last unveil."

Develop an infinite capacity to ignore what others think can't be done. Don't just grow where you are planted. Bloom where you are planted and bear fruit. Daniel Webster said, "There is always room at the top." No one can predict to what heights you can soar. Even you will not know until you spread your wings.

Know your limits, then ignore them!

Question 2

Who are the five people you spend the most time with? Are they increasing you or holding you back?

I received a phone call from a good friend and board member of my ministry, Tim Redmond. Tim wanted to meet with me and pick my brain. "I insist on paying for lunch, and I insist on paying you something for your time. What you know will really help me," he said. I must admit, I was a little uncomfortable charging anything because he is such a good friend.

We had our meeting and he asked some excellent questions. Tim is one of the brightest men I know, but what he was about to say to me would greatly impact me. I'll never forget his words: "Nobody has your experience. You've been the head of three publishing companies. You sold nearly two million books as an author. Think about how many people would like to talk to you about the book that's a dream in their heart. You would bring a perspective that no one else in Christian publishing could bring."

As I left our meeting and drove back to my office, Tim's words were still ringing in my heart and in my mind. I must say I'd never seriously considered how helpful and valuable my insights and experiences could be. I can tell you exactly where I was driving when I decided to make myself available to authors. To help them create their books. To help them publish their books. From that day forward, I have been constantly busy helping authors by simply making myself available to them. I don't think I ever would have had this idea without the words Tim said to me that day.

Isn't it incredibly important who we associate with? And who we let speak into our lives? God connects us with people because he loves people. Listen closely to those God has sent your way.

Tell me who your friends are, and I will tell you who you are. The simple but true fact of life is that you become like those you closely associate with—for the good and the bad.

The less you associate with some people, the more your life will improve. If you run with wolves, you will learn how to howl. But if you associate with eagles, you will learn how to soar to great heights. Almost all our sorrows spring out of relationships with the wrong people. E. K. Piper said, "Keep out of the suction caused by those who drift backwards."

Any time you tolerate mediocrity in others, it increases your mediocrity. We should pray, "Lord, deliver me from people who talk of nothing but despair and failure. Rather, grant me the companionship of those who think success and will work for it." A true Bulgarian proverb confirms, "If you find yourself taking two steps forward and one step back-wards, invariably it's because you have mixed associations in your life." If a loafer isn't a nuisance to you, it's a sign that you are somewhat of a loafer yourself. An important attribute in successful people is their impatience with negative thinking and negative-acting people.

A true friend is one who is there to care. It's been said a good friend is like one mind in two bodies. Robert Louis Stevenson said, "A friend is a gift you give yourself." You'll find a true friend remains a friend even when you don't deserve to have a friend. This person will see you through when others think that you're through.

The wisdom of Proverbs asserts, "Do not forsake your own friend or your father's friend, and do not go to your brother's house in the day of your calamity; better is a neighbor who is near than a brother far away" (27:10 NASB). Choose your associates carefully. This old saying is true: "He that lieth down with dogs shall rise up with fleas."

A true friend sees what you can be. Consider what Francesco Guicciardini said: "Since there is nothing so well worth having as friends, never lose a chance to make them."

Never become friends with someone because you both agree on negatives. Rather, find friends who agree with you on positives. "My best friend is the man who in wishing me well wishes it for my sake," Aristotle said. The Bible declares, "Iron sharpeneth iron; so a man sharpeneth the countenance of his friend" (Prov. 27:17). Thomas Carlyle observed, "Show me the man you honor, and I will know what kind of man you are, for it shows me what your ideal of manhood is, and what kind of man you long to be."

If you were to list your greatest benefits, resources, or strengths, you would find that money is one of the least important ones, while some of your greatest resources are the people you know. My friend Mike Murdock said, "Someone is always observing you who is capable of greatly blessing you." I believe that God blesses people through people. He has the right associations for you in your life.

A true friend is the best possession.

Question 3

If you're not you, then who are you going to be?

No matter where you go, one thing is certain—people are very different. I like to people watch, especially at airports. Every kind of shape, size, nationality, and culture is there. I can't help but be fascinated, wondering what people do or where they are headed and why. God made every one of us in a very particular way.

I've come to accept the fact that God knows a whole lot more than we do about why He put us together the way He did.

I sure would've liked to have been six feet four instead of five feet eight and have a full head of hair instead of a few remaining hairs. I was "blessed" to have five baby teeth that didn't have any permanent ones under them. I still have one holding on today. God even gave me a nice gap in the front of my teeth (think David Letterman). One of the funniest things I've experienced in my life is a poster I saw of myself in Monterrey, Mexico. The poster was promoting an event I was speaking at. It had a nice picture of me, the one we provided.

But there was something different about this picture. They had Photoshopped my gap! There I was, smiling, with a beautiful set of teeth with no front gap.

Why? I don't know. But I do know this: "If God had wanted me otherwise, He would have created me otherwise" (Goethe). Dare to be what you are. Resolve to be yourself. A Congolese proverb asserts, "Wood may remain ten years in the water, but it will never become a crocodile." The Bible asks, "Can the Ethiopian change his skin or the leopard his spots?" (Jer. 13:23 ESV). "Be what you are. This is the first step toward becoming better than you are," Julius Hare advised.

"My mother said to me, 'If you become a soldier, you'll become a general. If you become a monk, you'll end up as the pope.' Instead, I became a painter and wound up as Picasso," the great painter said. No one ever became great by imitation. Don't be a copy of something. Make your own impression.

"The curious paradox is that when I accept myself just as I am, then I can change," Carl Rogers said. Worn-out paths are for worn-out men. Friedrich Klopstock remarked, "He who has no opinion of his own, but depends on the opinion and taste of others, is a slave. To only dream of the person you are supposed to be is to waste the person you are." Nobody is so disappointed and so unhappy as the person who longs all of life to be somebody other than who they really are.

Those who trim themselves to suit everybody will soon whittle themselves away. If you don't have a plan for your own life, you'll only become a part of someone else's. You can't carry two faces under one hat. Never wish to be anything but what you are. "It is better to be hated for what you are than to be loved for what you are not," André Gide said.

"All the discontented people I know are trying sedulously to be something they are not, to do something they cannot do," David Grayson commented. When you will not dare to be yourself, you will lack confidence.

"Man is more interesting than men. God made him and not them in his image. Each one is more precious than all," André Gide reflected. "All good things which exist are the fruits of originality," John Mills said. There is only one life for each of us—our own. The person who walks in another's tracks never leaves their own footprints. Doris Mortman observed, "Until you make peace with who you are, you will never be content with what you have." Most of our challenges in life come from not knowing ourselves and ignoring our best, real virtues.

Most people live their entire lives as complete strangers to themselves. Don't let that happen to you. Leo Buscaglia counseled, "The easiest thing to be in the world is you. The most difficult thing to be is what other people want you to be. Don't let them put you in that position." The opposite of courage is not fear. It is conformity. The most exhausting and frustrating thing in life is to live it trying to be someone else.

Imitation is limitation.

Question 4

Does today feel different than yesterday?

Today should feel different than yesterday, if only in a very small way. Otherwise you're sitting still.

Change. I hope this word doesn't scare you but rather inspires you. Herbert Spencer said, "A living thing is distinguished from a dead thing by the multiplicity of the changes at any moment taking place in it." Change is an evidence of life. It is impossible to grow without change. Those who cannot change their minds cannot change anything. The truth is, life is always at some turning point.

I found myself at a turning point in 1992. I had accepted an invitation from several churches in Florida to speak in their services over a two-week period. In addition to those opportunities, I was also invited to speak at a monthly devotional held by a prominent publishing company. It was December, a great time to be in Florida.

At the publishing company, I had a great time and went to lunch right afterward with the leadership team and the owner's wife. I had no idea my life was about to change.

Within one day, I received a very pleasant phone call from the owner. They were looking for somebody to head their book publishing company. He wanted a change. The company had not been doing very well and was in desperate need of fresh leadership.

He wanted to meet me and have dinner as soon as possible. I had a good dinner and conversation with both him and his wife. It didn't take very long for him to begin to talk to me about coming to run his company. I had absolutely no desire to do that. In fact, I remember thinking, *This is a great way to interview for a job*. We ended our dinner that evening with him offering me a position. And me not being interested at all.

My wife, Linda, was flying out to Florida to join me the second week of my two-week tour. I was looking forward to her being there. The owner of the publishing company continued to reach out to me and asked to meet with both Linda and me about the job. I still was not interested, but out of respect to him (and maybe a free meal), I said okay.

Again, we had a great meeting and he continued to pursue me to run his company. Something began to change inside of me. I began to sense that God may be in this opportunity.

As I continued to travel and speak in Florida, the idea that God was calling me to help turn this company around became stronger and clearer. Change was about to happen in my life and in the life of my family.

I said yes, and within one month I found myself living in Florida, running that company.

What people want is progress—if they can have it without change. Impossible! You must change and recognize that change is your greatest ally. The person who never changes their opinion never corrects their mistakes. The fact is, the road to success is always under construction.

Yesterday's formula for success is often tomorrow's recipe for failure. Consider what Thomas Watson, the founder of the IBM Corporation, said in 1943: "There is a world market for about five computers." Where would IBM be today if Mr. Watson had not been willing to change?

You cannot become what you are destined to be by remaining what you are. John Patterson said, "Only fools and dead men don't change their minds. Fools won't. Dead men can't." If you don't respect the need for change, consider this: how many things have you seen change just in the past year?

When you change yourself, opportunities will change. The same kind of thinking that has brought you to where you are will not necessarily get you to where you want to go. Sainte-Beuve discovered this truth: "There are people whose watch stops at a certain hour and who remain permanently at that age."

Do not fear change; it's the law of progress. The man who uses yesterday's methods in today's world won't be in business tomorrow. A traditionalist is simply a person whose mind is always open to new ideas, provided they are the same old ones. "There are people who not only strive to remain static themselves, but strive to keep everything else so. . . . Their position is almost laughably hopeless," Odell Shepard said.

The unhappiest people are the ones who most fear change. When patterns and tradition are broken, new opportunities come together. Defending your faults and errors only proves that you have no intention of quitting them. All progress is due to those who were not satisfied to let well enough alone. They weren't afraid to change.

Change is not your enemy—it is your friend.

Would the child you were be proud of the man or woman you are?

What kind of impact do you want to leave? How will you be remembered? Most of us will never know what will be said at our funeral, but one man did.

Alfred Nobel, the inventor of dynamite, had a rude awakening when in 1888 a French newspaper printed his obituary. Thinking Alfred instead of his brother had died, the premature obituary was headed, "The Merchant of Death Is Dead."

Alfred was shocked, not only to read his own obituary but also to learn that he would be remembered in such a negative and destructive way. So in his will, he ordered his considerable estate to be invested and the interest awarded each year as prizes "to those persons who during the previous year have rendered the greatest service to mankind." We know this today as the Nobel Prize.

Alfred Nobel succeeded in transforming his image and his legacy.

How are you going to be remembered, and what will be the legacy you leave behind?

A four-year-old boy was asked to return thanks before Christmas dinner. The family members bowed their heads in expectation. He began his prayer by thanking God for all his friends, naming them one by one.

Then he thanked God for Mommy, Daddy, his brother and sister, Grandma, Grandpa, and all his aunts and uncles. Then he began to thank God for the food. He gave thanks for the turkey, the dressing, the fruit salad, the cranberry sauce, the pies, the cakes, even the Cool Whip.

Then he paused, and everyone waited . . . and waited. After a long silence, the young fellow looked up at his mother and asked, "If I thank God for the broccoli, won't He know I'm lying?"

Character is the real foundation of all worthwhile success. A good question to ask yourself is, "What kind of world would this be if everybody was just like me?" You are simply a book telling the world about its author. John Morley remarked, "No man can climb out beyond the limitations of his own character."

Some people try to make something for themselves. Others try to make something of themselves. Tryon Edwards said, "Thoughts lead on to purposes; purposes go forth in action; actions form habits; habits decide character; and character fixes our destiny." The Bible asserts in Proverbs 22:1, "A good name is rather to be chosen than great riches."

Never be ashamed of doing right. Marcus Aurelius exhorted, "Never esteem anything as of advantage to you that

will make you break your word or lose your self-respect."
W. J. Dawson counseled, "You need not choose evil; but only
to fail to choose good, and you drift fast enough towards evil.
You do not need to say, 'I will be bad,' you only have to say,
'I will not choose God's choice,' and the choice of evil is
already settled." There is no such thing as a *necessary evil*.
Phillips Brooks said, "A man who lives right and is right has
more power in his silence than another has by his words."

Many a man's reputation would not recognize his character
if they met in the dark. To change your character, you must
begin at the control center—the heart. Loss is inevitable when
a person is no longer able to keep the interest paid on their
moral obligations.

Henry Ward Beecher said, "No man can tell whether he is
rich or poor by turning to his ledger. It is the heart that makes
a man rich. He is rich according to what he is, not according
to what he has." Live so that your friends *can* defend you but
never *must* do so. Consider what Woodrow Wilson said: "If
you think about what you ought to do for other people, your
character will take care of itself." Excellence in character
is shown by doing unwitnessed what we would do with the
whole world watching.

Let me pose this question for you: Where do you compro-
mise? You should grow like a tree, not like a mushroom. It's
hard to climb high when your character is low. The world's
shortest sermon is preached by the traffic sign that says, "Keep
right."

> **Living a double life will get you
> nowhere twice as fast.**

Do you give space in your mind to those who don't want you to succeed?

An author and speaker I respect, Ron Ball, shared this from his *Ball Points* blog:

> According to a review in *The New Yorker* in 1939, the movie, *The Wizard of Oz*, "Displays no trace of imagination, good taste, or ingenuity. . . . It's a stinkeroo."
>
> A reviewer in *The New Republic* wrote about the film, *Jaws*, in 1975, "If sharks can yawn . . . that's presumably what this one is doing. It's certainly what I was doing all through this picture."
>
> *Current History* magazine printed this in 1938, "Snow White is a failure in every way. As a moving figure, she is unreal. As a face and body she is absurd. And what she does is ludicrous. . . . Another Snow White will sound the Disney death-knell."
>
> A writer in *Films in Review* wrote in 1956 of the star of the movie, *Love Me Tender*, "Elvis is a young man of hulk and

flabby muscle, with a degenerate face, who sings in emasculated innuendos. . . . How a society as dynamic as our own throws up such a monstrosity is beyond the scope of this review."

A critic in *New York* magazine recorded in 1977, in a review of the new film *Star Wars*, "O dull new world! It is all as exciting as last year's weather reports. . . . All trite characters and paltry verbiage."

National Review printed in 1980 that in *The Empire Strikes Back*, "Everything is stale, limp, desperately stretched out, and pretentious. Harrison Ford [as Han Solo] offers loutishness as charm."

You, of course, should learn what you can from your critics, but you should never let your critics get you down. Sometimes they are totally *wrong*.

It is easy to criticize and difficult to build. Remember that a critic may have missed who you are and what you are trying to accomplish.

Remember as well how you feel when someone tears you down, and decide not to do that to other people. If you need to evaluate someone, be nice. Be their friend, not their critic.

To succeed in life, you must overcome the many efforts of others to pull you down. How you choose to respond to criticism is one of the most important decisions you make.

The first and great commandment about critics is: *Don't let them scare you*. Charles Dodgson said, "If you limit your actions in life to things that nobody can possibly find fault with, you will not do much." Nothing significant has ever been accomplished without controversy, without criticism. When you allow other people's words to stop you, they will.

Christopher Morley said, "The truth is, a critic is like a gong at a railroad crossing, clanging loudly and vainly as the train goes by." Many great ideas have been lost because people who had them couldn't stand the criticism and gave up. One of the easiest things to find is fault. A critic is simply someone who finds fault without a search warrant. "The most insignificant people are the most apt to sneer at others. They are safe from reprisals. And have no hope of rising in their own esteem but by lowering their neighbors," William Hazlitt said. Critics not only expect the worst but make the worst of what happens.

Dennis Wholey warned, "Expecting the world to treat you fairly because you are a good person is like expecting the bull not to attack you because you are a vegetarian." I agree with Fred Allen when he said, "If criticism had any real power to harm, the skunk would have been extinct by now." Remember this about a critic: a person who is always kicking seldom has a leg to stand on. Great minds discuss ideas, good minds discuss events, and small minds discuss other people.

Don't allow yourself to become a critic. "Stop judging, so that you won't be judged" (Matt. 7:1 ISV). You will always make a mountain out of a molehill when you throw dirt at other people. No mud can soil you except for the mud you throw at others. The mud thrower never has clean hands.

You can't carve your way to success with cutting remarks. You will never move up if you are continually running someone down. I agree with John Tillotson: "There is no readier way for a man to bring his own worth into question than by endeavoring to detract from the worth of other men." Henry Ford commented, "Men and automobiles are much alike. Some are right at home on an uphill pull; others run smoothly only going downgrade. When you hear one knocking all the time, it's a sure sign there is something wrong under the hood."

If you are afraid of criticism, you will die doing nothing. If you want a place in the sun, you should expect some blisters and some sand kicked in your face. Criticism is a compliment when you know what you're doing is right.

> **When you make your mark in life, you will always attract erasers.**

Question 7

Why? Why not?
Why not you? Why not now?

I watched a heavy thunderstorm from the fifty-second floor of the building where I worked. I had just attended a dinner event with my wife, Linda, who was eight months pregnant. We were both ready to go home, so we ventured out to our car because it was only a light rain now, even though it had been quite an impressive storm.

We left downtown Tulsa and headed toward our home in the suburbs. When we were only a few miles away, I turned onto a road that crosses over a well-known creek. As I made the turn, I noticed the road was covered with water. It didn't look very deep, so I cautiously drove our car, a Volkswagen Beetle, into the water. Dumb idea.

Within moments, the water current substantially increased. We began to rock from side to side. The car began to float and moved toward the creek. I thought, *I've got my brand-new golf shoes in here, and they're going to be ruined as well as this car.* Linda was thinking, *I hope we don't go down into the creek and drown!*

It was a very serious situation. We offered a desperate prayer. Suddenly, our car became lodged off the road in an area just a short distance from the turbulent creek.

I decided we needed to get out of that car, fast, before it became dislodged. I told Linda to roll down her window—the water was now at that level. Linda amazingly squeezed through the window and I did the same, grabbing my golf shoes on the way out.

As we were wading up the current, an emergency services worker greeted us and began to assist us to higher ground.

I started with a wrong decision driving into that water, but ended with the life-saving decision that caused us to get out of it as soon as possible.

Most of our decisions are not as dramatic as this. But sometimes a seemingly unimportant decision becomes one of the most important we can make. Successful people make decisions, even if it means they'll sometimes be wrong.

"My decision is maybe—and that's final." Does this sound like you? Being decisive is essential for a successful life. If you deny yourself commitment, what will you do with your life? Every accomplishment, great or small, starts with a decision.

Choice, not chance, determines destiny. You can't get a hit with the bat on your shoulder. Nothing great is ever done without an act of decision. Too many people go through life not knowing what they want but feeling sure they don't have it. Herbert Prochnow said, "There is a time when we must firmly choose the course which we will follow, or the relentless drift of events will make the decision for us."

Too many people are like wheelbarrows, trailers, or canoes. They need to be pushed, pulled, or paddled. Either you're moving other people to decisions or they're moving you. Decide to do something now to make *your* life better. The choice is yours.

David Ambrose remarked, "If you have the will to win, you have achieved half your success; if you don't, you have achieved half your failure." Lou Holtz said, "If you don't make a total commitment to whatever you are doing, then you start looking to bail out the first time the boat starts leaking. It's tough enough getting the boat to shore with everybody rowing, let alone when a guy stands up and starts putting his life jacket on."

The moment you commit yourself, God moves too. All sorts of things happen to help you that never would have otherwise occurred. Edgar Roberts said, "Every human mind is a great slumbering power until awakened by a keen desire and a definite resolution to do." Kenneth Blanchard observed, "There is a difference between interest and commitment. When you're interested in doing something, you only do it when it is convenient. When you're committed to something, you accept no excuses, only results." Lack of decisiveness has caused more failures than lack of intelligence or ability.

Maurice Switzer said, "You seldom get what you go after unless you know in advance what you want." Our indecision often gives an advantage to another person because they did their thinking beforehand. Helen Keller said, "Science may have found a cure for most evils; but it has found no remedy for the worst of them all—the apathy of human beings." Joshua 24:15 encourages us, "Choose for yourselves this day whom you will serve" (NIV). Don't leave a decision for tomorrow that needs to be made today.

Bertrand Russell said, "Nothing is so exhausting as indecision, and nothing is so futile." Joseph Newton discerned, "Not what we have, but what we use, not what we see, but what we choose, these are the things that mar or bless the sum of human happiness." Don't be a middle-of-the-roader, because the middle of the road is the worst place to try to go forward. You can do everything you ought to do once you make a decision. Today, decide on your dream.

> **There's nothing in the middle of the road but yellow stripes and dead armadillos.** (James Hightower)

Question 8

If you could, what would you work on right now?

I started my first business at age twelve. It wasn't my idea but my dad's. He even helped me get a business card that said, "Lawn mowing. Weekly or as needed."

For the next four years, I would cut approximately eight yards a week. Many of those were for doctors' offices and businesses located along a busy highway. I still remember many days riding my bicycle, one hand on the handlebar holding the bicycle and a broom, the other hand pulling the mower along as I rode on to my next customer. I made and saved a decent amount of money for college doing this. I later ended up selling my little lawn mowing business to a neighborhood kid for a couple hundred dollars. But the most important thing I learned early on was how to work. And how important work is.

You can't fulfill your destiny on a theory. It takes *work*. You are made for action. It is much more natural for you to be doing than sitting. Success simply takes good ideas and puts them into action. What the *free enterprise* system means is that the more enterprising you are, the freer you are. What this country needs is less emphasis on *free* and more on *enterprise*.

Listen to Shakespeare: "Nothing can come of nothing." A belief is worthless unless converted into action. The word *work* is not an obscure concept; it appears in the Bible over five hundred times. Often, the simple answer to your prayer is: *Go to work*.

David Bly said, "Striving for success without hard work is like trying to harvest where you haven't planted." What you believe doesn't amount to very much unless it causes you to climb out of the grandstand and onto the playing field. You cannot just dream yourself into what you could be. The only time a lazy person ever succeeds is when he tries to do nothing. Benjamin Franklin says it best: "Laziness travels so slowly, poverty soon overtakes him."

A person who wastes enormous amounts of time talking about success will win the "prize" of failure. When you are lazy, you must work twice. It is always a trying time for the person who is constantly attempting to get something for nothing. God doesn't make apple juice—He makes apples. Some say *nothing* is impossible, yet there are a lot of people doing *nothing* every day.

Some do things, while others sit around becoming experts on how things might be done. The world is divided into people who do things and people who talk about doing things. Belong to the first group—there is far less competition.

We're not burdened with work. We're blessed with it. "Men are all alike in their promises. It is only in their deeds that they differ," Molière said. Wishing has never made a poor

41

man wealthy. Robert Half nailed it: "Laziness is the secret ingredient that goes into failure, but it's only kept a secret from the person who fails."

Tell yourself what Brendan Francis said: "Inspirations never go in for long engagements; they demand immediate marriage to action." If the truth were known, most of our troubles arise from loafing when we should be working, and talking when we should be listening.

> **None of the secrets of success will work unless you do.**

Question 9

What's your favorite excuse? Why are you still using it?

I spent a number of my early years as a consultant to churches. I would help them with strategic planning, job descriptions, marketing, salary issues, and many other practical areas of ministry.

One of the things I always tried to do with a new client was to sit in their Sunday morning service. Because this is their main "product," I looked forward to experiencing it firsthand. I also wanted to play a kind of "secret shopper." In other words, I would come in and see how I was greeted, how easy it was to know where to drop the children off, how the sound was in the sanctuary, and many other things.

I'll never forget one church I was helping that had a very tall worship leader. In fact, he was six feet seven. At this Sunday morning service, the pastor, associate pastor, and worship leader all sat on the platform facing the members. The service started and the worship began. This church did not use hymnals; rather, an overhead projector displayed the words to each song on the wall behind the worship leader.

I watched closely and noticed that because the worship leader was so tall, the projection had to be moved up the wall. So the first two or three lines of every song ended up on the ceiling. The people wouldn't sing on those lines but only on the lines that showed up on the wall.

After the morning service, the pastor, his team, and I went to lunch. They asked me questions about the service and we began to discuss everything that went on. I asked, "Have you noticed the congregation doesn't begin to sing until they get to the third or fourth line of the song?"

"Yes!" both the pastor and the worship leader exclaimed. "We've been working so hard to get the congregation to participate at the start of every song. We've tried new songs, we've tried very familiar songs, we've tried popular songs, but nothing seems to help. They don't begin to sing at all until the third or fourth line of every song!" I could tell they were pretty upset with their church members.

I couldn't help but smile and think how they were actually paying money for the advice I was about to give them. I looked at them and said, "Do you know they have to place the first two or three lines of every song on the ceiling because your worship leader is so tall?"

They had no idea. They were pursuing every reason (or maybe every excuse) without considering they might be part of the problem. The pastor and I still chuckle about that funny day nearly thirty years later.

You treat others right when you don't blame them for anything that is actually wrong with you. "Never mind whom you praise, but be very careful whom you blame," Edmund Gosse said. You can fall down many times, but you won't be a failure until you say that someone else pushed you.

When it comes to excuses, the world is full of great inventors. Some spend half their lives telling what they are going to do, and others spend half their lives explaining why they didn't do it. An alibi is the proof that you did do what you didn't do, so that others will think you didn't do what you did.

You can fail many times but not be a failure until you begin to blame someone else. Our own mistakes fail in their mission of helping us when we blame them on other people. When you use excuses, you give up your power to change.

If you can find an excuse, don't use it. Most failures are experts at making excuses. There are always enough available if you are weak enough to use them. The world simply does not have enough crutches for all the lame excuses. It's always easier to find excuses instead of time for the things we don't want to do.

So find a way—there is no excuse for a human being full of excuses. Someone who makes a mistake and then makes an excuse for it is making two mistakes. Note this truth from William Blake: "The fox condemns the trap, not himself." Don't find yourself talking like that old fox!

Never complain and never explain. "Admitting errors clears the score and proves you wiser than before," Arthur Guiterman said. Doing a job right is always easier than fabricating an alibi for why you didn't. Time wasted thinking up excuses and alibis will always be better spent praying, planning, preparing, and working toward your goals in life.

> **The most unprofitable item
> ever manufactured is an excuse.**

Question 10

What is something you can do for someone who has no opportunity to repay you?

Don't you just love the fact that God knows your future? And that He sends people into your present because He knows what you need in the years and decades ahead? God did that for me as a young high school student.

I remember one day my dad telling me that he had something he wanted me to get involved in. I was like most kids—resistant to anything a parent wants them to do, especially if it didn't involve sports or eating.

My dad had met a man name Bob Leiman, and they had become friends. Bob was an assistant principal at a local high school as well as a professional speaker. He had come up with a unique idea he wanted to start. It would be best described as a Junior Toastmasters Club for high school students. He called it "Junior Optimist."

My dad was very familiar with Toastmasters and thought I could benefit from learning how to speak in front of people. I had absolutely no interest in it whatsoever.

I grudgingly went with my dad to that first meeting. It was a Tuesday night, and the meeting was held at an old YMCA in downtown Fort Wayne, Indiana. We navigated through the dark and dank hallways to a room where the meeting was to be held. We opened the door and there was no one there. A big smile came to my face. I was very happy it was empty.

We soon learned that we had showed up on the wrong day. The meeting was Thursday, not Tuesday. So Thursday night my dad took me downtown again to attend this Junior Optimist meeting. It was there I met Bob Leiman. And it was there I was about to learn some things that would bless me and, humbly, hundreds of thousands of others for the rest of my life.

I participated in the club like all the other people, but Bob seemed to take a personal interest in me. He began to talk to me about speaking outside of the club. He took me places to be a speaker myself. I would speak at Lions clubs, Rotary clubs, Optimists clubs, and many other civic gatherings. I probably missed more than thirty lunches in high school because I was out speaking.

Soon doors began to open for me to enter speech contests, and I found myself winning several. Finishing second in the nation in a speech contest sponsored by *Reader's Digest* and the Boy Scouts of America was particularly memorable. All of this was directly traceable to my dad forcing me to go to these meetings, and to Bob Leiman helping, believing in, and training me.

Although there was nothing in it for Bob, he wanted to help someone else. Since that time, I've given hundreds of speeches to hundreds of thousands of people. Thank you, Dad and Bob.

If you are only looking out for yourself, look out! Wesley Huber said, "There is nothing quite so dead as a self-centered man—a man who holds himself up as a self-made success, and measures himself by himself and is pleased with the result." Is your favorite letter *I*? The only reason pride lifts you up is to let you down.

Norman Vincent Peale observed, "The man who lives for himself is a failure. Even if he gains much wealth, position, or fortune, he is still a failure." Conceit makes us fools. "Do you see a man wise in his own eyes? There is more hope for a fool than for him" (Prov. 26:12 NASB). The man who believes in nothing but himself lives in a very small world. The best way to be happy is to forget yourself and focus on other people. Henry Courtney said, "The bigger a man's head gets, the easier it is to fill his shoes." A swelled head always proves there is plenty of room for improvement.

"The greatest magnifying glasses in the world are a man's own eyes when they look upon his own person," Alexander Pope said. Egotism is the only disease where the patient feels well while making everyone else around them feel sick. It blossoms but bears no fruit. Those who sing their own praises seldom receive an encore. Charles Elliot intoned, "Don't think too much of yourself. Try to cultivate the habit of thinking of others; this will reward you. Selfishness always brings its own revenge."

When you are on a high horse, the best thing to do is dismount at once. You can't push yourself forward by patting yourself on the back. Burton Hillis remarked, "It's fine to believe in ourselves, but we mustn't be too easily convinced." An egotist is his own best friend. The fellow who is deeply in love with himself should get a divorce.

Folks who boast of being self-made usually have a few parts missing. You can recognize a self-made man; his head is oversized and he has arms long enough to pat himself on the back. Conceited people never get anywhere because they think they are already there.

Let's change our favorite word from "I" to "you."

> **Even postage stamps become useless
> when they get stuck on themselves.**

What progress are you standing in the way of?

An elderly woman walked into the local country church. The friendly usher greeted her at the door and helped her up the flight of steps.

"Where would you like to sit?" he asked politely.

"The front row, please," she answered.

"You really don't want to do that," the usher said. "The pastor is really boring."

"Do you happen to know who I am?"

"No."

"I'm the pastor's mother," she replied indignantly.

"Do you know who I am?"

"No."

"Good," he answered.

We should do everything we can to stay out of our own way. Stewart Johnson said, "Our business in life is not to get ahead of others, but to get ahead of ourselves—to break our own records, to outstrip our yesterdays by today, to do our work with more force than ever before." If you would like to know who is responsible for most of your troubles, look in the mirror. If you could kick the fellow responsible for most of your problems, you wouldn't be able to sit down for three weeks. It's time for us to stay out of our own way.

Most of the stumbling blocks people complain about are under their own hats. Louis XIV commented, "There is little that can withstand a man who can conquer himself." The Bible's wisdom counsels, "He that hath no rule over his own spirit is like a city that is broken down, and without walls" (Prov. 25:28).

"Your future depends on many things, but mostly on you," Frank Tyger said. You may succeed if nobody else believes in you, but you will never succeed if you don't believe in yourself. Zig Ziglar observed, "What you picture in your mind, your mind will go to work to accomplish. When you change your pictures you automatically change your performance." Whatever you attach consistently to the words "I am," you will become.

Ralph Waldo Emerson said, "It is impossible for man to be cheated by anyone but himself." Gain control of your mind or it will gain control of you. Your imagination dictates your openness to positive direction. As Norman Vincent Peale remarked, "Do not build up obstacles in your imagination. Remind yourself that God is with you and that nothing can defeat Him."

"Our best friends and our worst enemies are the thoughts we have about ourselves," Dr. Frank Crane said. Stop looking only at where you are and start looking at what you can be. The Bible declares, "For as he thinketh in his heart, so is he"

(Prov. 23:7). Be careful of your thoughts. They may become words at any moment and actions very soon. Wrong thinking almost always leads to misery.

No one can defeat you unless you first defeat yourself. Self-image sets the boundaries and limits of each of our individual accomplishments. Charles Colton said, "We are sure to be losers when we quarrel with ourselves; it is a civil war." If you doubt yourself, listen to Alexandre Dumas: "A person who doubts himself is like a man who would enlist in the ranks of his enemy and bears arms against himself." Tim Redmond advised, "Don't commit treason against your own life and purpose."

Your world first exists within you. Marion Crawford said, "Every man carries with him the world in which he must live." Having trouble hearing from God? According to Bob Harrison, "When God speaks, your mind will be your biggest enemy." Facing major obstacles in life? James Allen observed, "You are the handicap you must face. You are the one who must choose your place." Remember you are your own doctor when it comes to curing cold feet, a hot head, and a stuffy attitude.

Get ahead of yourself.

Question 12

What lies are you believing today?

One of the biggest lies we believe is what we conclude when we compare ourselves to others. It's never fair to compare.

The challenge is that we're seeing someone else's "play of the day" from the viewpoint of our daily grind. What makes us discontented is the silly belief that others are so much happier than we are.

In a powerful Cherokee legend about two wolves, an elderly chief was teaching his grandson about life. "A fight is going on inside me," he said to the boy. "It is a terrible fight and it is between two wolves. One is evil. He is anger, envy, sorrow, regret, greed, arrogance, self-pity, guilt, resentment, inferiority, lies, false pride, superiority, self-doubt, and ego.

"The other is good. He is joy, peace, hope, serenity, humility, kindness, benevolence, empathy, generosity, truth, compassion, and faith. The same fight is going on inside you, and inside every other person too."

The grandson thought about it for a minute and then asked, "Which wolf will win?"

The chief simply replied, "The one you feed."

We always have a choice as to how we will react to an event or action. Our response is determined by whichever wolf we feed.

Envy is the most ridiculous of ideas, for there is no single advantage to be gained from it. As a famous old saying goes, "When you compare what you want with what you have, you will be unhappy. Instead, compare what you deserve with what you have, and you'll discover happiness."

It's not trying to keep up with the Joneses that causes so much trouble. It's trying to pass them. Washington Allston reflected, "The only competition worthy of a wise mind is within himself." Nothing gets you behind faster than trying to keep up with people who are already there. And this is also true: *nothing* is as it appears.

If envy were a disease, everyone would be sick. Francis Bacon said, "Envy has no holidays. It has no rest." The envy by which we compare ourselves to others is foolishness. "They are only comparing themselves with each other, using themselves as the standard of measurement. How ignorant!" (2 Cor. 10:12 NLT).

Envy is one of the subtlest forms of judging others. Richard Evans said, "May we never let the things we can't have, or don't have, or shouldn't have, spoil our enjoyment of the things we do have and can have." What makes us discontented with our personal condition is the absurd belief that others are so much happier than we are. Thomas Fuller said, "Comparison, more than reality, makes men happy or wretched."

Helen Keller said, "Instead of comparing our lot with that of those who are more fortunate than we are, we should compare it with the lot of the great majority of our fellow men. It then appears that we are among the privileged." Envy consumes nothing but its own heart. It is a kind of admiration for those whom you least want to praise.

An Irish proverb says, "You've got to do your own growing, no matter how tall your grandfather was." You'll find it's hard to be happier than others if you believe others to be happier than they are. Worry about what other people think of you and you'll have more confidence in their opinion than in your own. Poor is the one whose pleasures depend on the permission and opinion of others.

Saint Chrysostom reflected, "As a moth gnaws a garment, so doth envy consume a man." If envy had a shape, it would be a boomerang. There are many roads to an unsuccessful life, but envy is one of the shortest of them all.

Comparison and envy, more than reality, make people happy or sad.

Question 13

Is this your very best?

A public high school in Queensland, Australia, has this voice-mail message when you call the school:

Hello! You have reached the automated answering service of your school. In order to assist you in connecting to the right staff member, please listen to all the options before making a selection:

To lie about why your child is absent—press 1.
To make excuses for why your child did not do his or her work—press 2.
To complain about what we do—press 3.
To swear at staff members—press 4.
To ask why you didn't get information that was already enclosed in your newsletter and several flyers mailed to you—press 5.
If you want us to raise your child—press 6.
If you want to reach out and touch, slap, or hit someone—press 7.
To request another teacher for the third time this year—press 8.
To complain about bus transportation—press 9.
To complain about school lunches—press 0.

If you realize this is the real world and your child must be accountable and responsible for his or her own behavior, class work, and homework, and that it's not the teachers' fault for your child's lack of effort—hang up and have a nice day!

We can learn a lot from this message. Living a life of excellence is up to us.

Richard Huseman said, "Be driven by excellence. To be driven by excellence so at the end of each day, each month, each year, and indeed at the end of life itself we must ask one important question: Have we demanded enough of ourselves, and by our example, inspired those around us to put forth their best effort and achieve their greatest potential?"

More harm has been done by weak persons than by wicked persons. The problems of this world have been caused by the weakness of goodness rather than by the strength of evil. The true measure of a person is in the height of their ideals, the breadth of their sympathy, the depth of their convictions, and the length of their patience.

Eddie Rickenbacker encouraged us, "Think positively and masterfully, with confidence and faith, and life becomes more secure, more fraught with action, richer in achievement and experience." You achieve according to what you believe.

"Of all the paths a man could strike onto, there is, at any given moment, a best path . . . a thing which, here and now, if it were of all things wisest for him to do . . . to find this path and walk in it, is the one thing needful for him," Thomas Carlyle reflected. The right train of thought will take you to a better station in life.

To try to do what's best and to remain essentially ourselves are really one and the same thing. Coach John Wooden said, "Success is peace of mind, which is a direct result of knowing you did your best to become the best that you are capable of becoming." One secret of success is being able to put your best foot forward without stepping on anybody's toes.

If you seek for greatness, then forget greatness and ask for God's will. You will find both. Harold Taylor said, "The roots of true achievement lie in the will to become the best that you can become." Elevate your personal standards of quality. Whatever you thought was good enough for now, add 10 percent more. Better is better.

The biggest mistake you can make in life is not to be true to the best you know. George Bernard Shaw remarked, "Keep yourself clean and bright; you are the window through which you must see the world." Follow Ralph Sockman's advice: "Give the best that you have to the highest you know—and do it now."

The time is always right to do the right thing.

Question 14

Which is worse—failing or never trying?

Sometimes I feel I'm an authority on failures and mistakes. I have so much experience.

Years ago I was invited to speak at a church I had never been to for a pastor I had never met. I had an early morning flight, so I was up before the break of dawn to finish my packing. I put everything in my suitcase and rushed off to the airport.

After thirty minutes in the air I began to replay my morning, checking off in my mind everything I had packed. Suit? Check. Shirts? Check. Shoes? Check.

Suddenly I wondered, *Did I bring my notes?* Yes. *My Bible?* Wait . . . I wasn't sure. I immediately looked inside my carry-on bag. No Bible! It was nowhere to be found, no matter how many times I searched my bag.

I felt slightly panicked. Here I was, flying to a new church led by a pastor I'd never met. I didn't want to walk off the plane, introduce myself, and then say, "Pastor, may I borrow your Bible?" I could only imagine him thinking, *Who have I entrusted my Sunday service to?*

I had to do something about this situation. I came up with what I thought was a good idea: I would find a bookstore in the airport and buy a Bible. But then I thought what you're probably thinking: *I've never seen a Bible for sale in the airport.* I began to get desperate.

I deplaned as fast as I could and made a beeline for the first store I could find selling books. "Do you sell Bibles?" I asked hopefully. "No" was the immediate response. I hurried to find another store and asked for a Bible. Again, the answer was no, but the clerk offered me some hope. She said, "I think the bookstore in the other terminal sells Bibles, so you should go there."

By then I should have been in baggage claim picking up my luggage, but I decided to run over to the other terminal in one last desperate attempt to secure a Bible. I passed gate after gate before I saw a bookstore. I headed straight for the cashier and, slightly out of breath, asked, "Do you sell Bibles?"

"Yes, we do," she cheerfully replied. "Let me go get one for you." Relieved, I waited. Only a minute later, she reappeared and handed me a small, white, baptismal-type gift Bible. I thought, *I didn't pack a white suit, white shirt, white tie, and white shoes. I can't preach from this little white Bible!* But I was desperate, so I went ahead and purchased it.

I quickly left the terminal and went down the escalator toward baggage claim, hoping to see a "pastor-looking" person. As I got to the bottom of the escalator, I saw a man alone, looking all around. I knew I had found him.

I went straight up to him and introduced myself. He said, "Thank goodness it's you! Here's your bag—it was the only one left."

We walked to his car and left the airport. Five minutes into our ride he asked, "Would you like to go to the church before the hotel? I'd like to show you our latest addition."

Usually I'd rather just head to my room, but then I thought, *A church! They'll have Bibles!* I enthusiastically replied, "Yes!"

Before long we arrived at the church, and I made it a point to follow just a little behind the pastor. As we were about to enter the beautiful sanctuary, I spotted a box to my left. On it was a "Lost and Found" sign.

My heart began to beat a little faster. I was hoping my search was over with my dignity still intact. Following the pastor, I walked beside the box and looked inside. There it was, a beautiful Bible! In one smooth motion I reached in and "found" that Bible.

That whole weekend I preached with "my" new Bible. But in the back of my mind I wondered if someone out in the congregation was thinking, *That guy's got my Bible!*

Before I left the church, I discreetly returned the Bible to the lost and found. What a happy find that Bible was!

We all make mistakes. Some are funny, some affect us for a lifetime.

To expect life to be perfectly tailored to our specifications is to live a life of continual frustration. When you make mistakes, just learn from them and don't respond with encores. George Bernard Shaw said, "A life spent making mistakes is not only more honorable, but more useful than a life spent doing nothing."

David McNally mused, "The mistake-riddled life is much richer, more interesting, and more stimulating than the life that has never risked or taken a stand on anything." According to Tom Hopkins, "The single most important difference between champion achievers and average people is their ability to handle rejection and failure." Listen to S. I. Hayakawa: "Notice the difference between what happens when a man says to himself, 'I have failed three times,' and what happens when he says, 'I am a failure.'" Failure is a situation, never a person.

Mistakes are often the best teachers. The Bible says in Ecclesiastes 7:14, "In the day of prosperity be joyful, but in the day of adversity consider." Oswald Avery advises, "Whenever you fall, pick something up." The man who invented the eraser had humanity well sized up. You will find that people who never make mistakes never make anything else. It's true: you can profit from your mistakes. That's why I am convinced I'll be a millionaire.

Failure is not falling down but staying down. Be like Jonah, who proved that you can't keep a good man down. Proverbs 24:16 reads, "For though a righteous man falls seven times, he will rise again" (ISV). Herman Melville wrote, "He who has never failed somewhere, that man can not be great."

The person who never makes a mistake takes orders from and lives his life for someone who does. Frederick Robertson related, "No man ever progressed to greatness and goodness but through great mistakes." William Ward said, "Failure is delay, but not defeat. It is a temporary detour, not a dead-end street."

Thomas Edison reflected, "People are not remembered by how few times they failed, but by how often they succeed."

Every wrong step can lead to another step forward. David Burns said, "Assert your right to make a few mistakes. If people can't accept your imperfection, that's their fault."

Louis Boone said, "Don't fear failure so much that you refuse to try new things. The saddest summary of a life contains three descriptions: could have, might have, and should have." Robert Schuller wrote, "Always look at what you have left. Never look at what you have lost." If you learn from them, mistakes are useful. Cultivate this attitude and you will never be ashamed to try. Uncover the jewels from your mistakes.

> **You can't travel the road to success**
> **without a puncture or two.**

Question 15

What are you really aiming at?

A woman walked into my wife's and my life at a very strategic time. No one else knew it, but Linda and I were planning to move from Florida back to Tulsa. We had many conversations about what kind of house we wanted and where we specifically wanted to live.

After attending a service, this woman we knew and respected came up to us and said, "I believe in my heart that I have something to share with you from the Lord." She began to say how God knew what was on our hearts and that we were to write it out and gather the information. She even said to cut out pictures of what the desire of our hearts was, and that God was going to give it to us. We knew this specific word was for the house we were seeking.

I was encouraged by this. But Linda took the woman's words to a completely different level. She began to create a notebook full of pictures and diagrams of exactly the house she wanted. She detailed how many bedrooms she wanted, where she wanted them located, how many fireplaces, what the yard should look like, basically where everything would be in the house. That is one thing I love about my wife—she will do exactly what God shows her to do.

I had to take a trip to Tulsa for business and Linda was unable to go with me. After I was done with business there, I decided to look at some houses. I spent the whole day looking at homes with our Realtor, but none stood out for me. And I knew that none looked like the house Linda was creating in her folder.

At the end of a long day I decided to go out to my friend Tim Redman's home to have dinner with him and his wife, Sandy. As I was driving to their house and was less than a tenth of a mile away, I noticed a neighborhood that I'd never seen before. It was a little early for dinner, so I decided to turn into the community and check it out.

The neighborhood was full of beautiful homes, quite a ways beyond what I thought we could afford. There were only thirteen homes in one big circle. I rounded the turn and saw a house that had a "For Sale by Builder" sign in front of it. I hesitated about approaching the door because of the size of the property and the home. But I thought I might as well check it out.

I rang the doorbell. A man answered and immediately said, "John Mason, what are you doing here in Tulsa? I thought you moved to Florida." What a surprise to know the builder! I chuckled and said I did live in Florida, but I was considering moving back and interested in knowing a little bit more about the house.

He welcomed me into the home. Before we began to tour it, I told him that my wife was not with me and that I would need her to look at anything before we made any decisions.

He said that was no problem. In fact, he would videotape the entire house as we walked through so I could show it to her when I returned to Florida.

It was a beautiful, brand-new home. The builder was living in it for a few months until he could sell it. As I walked through the house, I thought, *This has a lot of things that Linda likes and that she's been writing down.*

As I left the house after the tour, I said to the owner, "I'm not sure I can afford this house, but I do like it." He began to tell me about a special builder's loan he had on the house that was assumable, which might make the deal work for me. I left there interested but unsure. It was almost too good to be true.

I went straight to my friend Tim's house and we began to eat dinner together. I shared with him and Sandy about the house for sale nearby. As I talked, Tim's eyes got bigger and bigger. He said, "I know that house! I've been to it on many occasions as they were building it, and for some reason I felt led to walk around the house and pray over it and *call it into the ministry.*"

Now we all began to get excited about this house. A couple days later, I flew home to Linda. As soon as we could, we played the videotape of the house. As we went from room to room, inside and outside the house, we got more and more excited. She opened her folder and began to show me what she had written and what she wanted in the house. And this house matched what she had written exactly, down to the smallest detail. God had the right place for us. We purchased that house and happily lived in it for nearly twenty years.

God has a right place for you. It will take focus. It will take commitment. It will take persistence. It will take faith. It will require action.

William Locke said, "I can tell how to get what you want; you just got to keep a thing in view and go for it, and never let your eyes wander to the right or left or up or down. And looking back is fatal." Jesus warns, "No man can serve two masters: for either he will hate the one, and love the other; or else he will hold to the one, and despise the other" (Matt. 6:24). When you serve two masters, you must lie to one.

Do *more* by doing *less*. Delegate, simplify, or eliminate low priorities as soon as possible. James Liter said, "One thought driven home is better than three left on base."

There are too many people in too many cars, in too much of a hurry, going too many directions, to get nowhere for nothing. "There is so little time for the discovery of all that we want to know about things that really interest us. We cannot afford to waste it on things that are only of casual concern for us, or in which we are interested only because other people have told us what we ought to be," Alec Waugh said. For the person who has no focus, there is no peace.

Tim Redmond said, "Don't be a jack of all trades and a master of none. Instead be like the apostle Paul who wrote, 'This one thing I do . . . I press toward the mark.'" What you set your heart on will determine how you will spend your life. Carl Sandberg said, "There are people who want to be everywhere at once, and they get nowhere."

George Bernard Shaw wrote, "Give a man health and a course to steer, and he'll never stop to trouble about whether he is happy or not." We know that Walt Disney was successful. Maybe the key to his success is found in his confession: "I love Mickey Mouse more than any woman I've ever known." Now that's focus!

Vic Braden said, "Losers have tons of variety. Champions take pride in just learning to hit the same old boring winning shots." Consider what George Robson said after winning the Indianapolis 500: "All I had to do was keep turning left."

I believe you will only find happiness when you are in a position of going somewhere wholeheartedly, in one direction, without regret or reservation. Do what you are doing while you are doing it. The more complicated you are, the more ineffective you will become.

Mark Twain said, "Behold, the fool saith, 'Put not all thine eggs in one basket' — which is but a manner of saying, 'Scatter your money and your attention.' But the wise man saith, 'Put all your eggs in the one basket and — watch that basket.'" The quickest way to do many things is to do only one thing at a time. The only people who will be remembered are those who have done one thing superbly well. Don't be like the man who said, "I'm focused, it's just on something else."

> **If you chase two rabbits, both will escape.** (Anonymous)

Do you take the advice of your fears?

I have had six knee surgeries. I don't recommend even one for you. It all started with a noncontact injury that tore my cartilage while I played intramural football in college. Over the years, after surgery upon surgery, the cartilage got worse, to the point that I needed a knee replacement.

The doctors in charge told me I wouldn't get the same results as most people because my knee coming into surgery was in such terrible shape. But I obviously needed it, so I went ahead with the replacement surgery.

My initial results the first few days were good. I seemed to be progressing just fine. Then incredible pain began in my knee and on my leg. It was getting worse and worse. The pain was so intense that I literally could not even have the sheets on my bed touch my leg. I continued to see my surgeon, and it wasn't long thereafter that he diagnosed me with an unusual problem called complex regional pain syndrome, sometimes also known as reflex sympathetic dystrophy, or RSD. It seems that a very small percentage of people who have knee replacement get this terrible disorder.

The trouble persisted for nearly two months. I was on the strongest painkillers possible. They were messing with my mind and only barely helping with the pain. I began to wonder, sometimes out loud, if I would ever walk again. Fear was trying to take hold of me. I had never felt so low and afraid.

But like He always does, God brought answers. I became connected with an outstanding pain management doctor. She began to treat me with spinal blocks and therapy, and eventually I began to get better. Today I can walk. My knee is not perfect, but I'm thankful I can get around. One thing is for certain—worry and fear never make you better.

Never trouble trouble until trouble troubles you. Arthur Roche said, "Worry is a thin stream of fear trickling through the mind. If encouraged, it cuts a channel into which all other thoughts are drained." Instead, do what Dr. Rob Gilbert advised: "It's all right to have butterflies in your stomach. Just get them to fly in formation."

Only your mind can produce fear. Jesus said, "Which of you by worrying can add one cubit to his stature?" (Matt. 6:27 NKJV). We choose our joys and our fears long before we experience them. I agree with Helen Keller: "It gives me a deep, comforting sense that things seen are temporal and things unseen are eternal." George Porter said, "Always be on guard against your imagination. How many lions it creates in our paths, and so easily! And we suffer so much if we do not turn a deaf ear to its tales and suggestions."

Fears, like babies, grow larger by nursing them. Fear wants to grow faster than a teenager. Benjamin Disraeli said, "Nothing in life is more remarkable than the unnecessary anxiety which we endure, and generally create ourselves." We must act despite fear—not because of it. If you are afraid to step up to the plate, you will never hit a home run.

Sister Mary Tricky said, "Fear is faith that it won't work out." The Bible says in Psalm 46:1–2, "God is our refuge and strength, a very present help in trouble. Therefore we will not fear" (ESV). Don't fear, for the Lord is with you. If you ask for His help, He will never leave you to face your challenges alone.

Lucy Montgomery said, "It only seems as if you are doing something when you are worrying." Worry doesn't help tomorrow's troubles, but it does ruin today's happiness. "A day of worry is more exhausting than a week of work," John Lubbock mused. When you worry about the future, there will soon be no future for you to worry about. No matter how much a person dreads the future, he usually wants to be around to see it. The truth is, more people worry about the future than prepare for it.

Shakespeare wrote, "Our doubts are traitors and make us lose the good we oft might win by fearing to attempt." Emanuel Celler said, "Don't roll up your pant legs before you get to the stream."

"If you are distressed by anything external, the pain is not due to the thing itself, but to your estimate of it; and this you have the power to revoke at any moment," Marcus Aurelius reflected. Fears lie and keep us from going where we might have found victory. There are always two voices

71

sounding in our ears—the voice of fear and the voice of faith. One is the clamor of the senses. The other is the whispering of God. Never let your fears hold you back from pursuing your dream.

Worry never fixes anything.

Question 17

Whom do you need to forgive today?

Be strong. Forgive someone who isn't sorry. Accept the apology you'll never receive. Before you hate someone else, stop and remember all that God has forgiven you for.

Probably one of the bravest and most remarkable women in history was Corrie ten Boom. She risked her life to save the lives of others by harboring Jews during the Holocaust. However, due to an informant, she and her family were arrested, ending in the death of her father. Her sister also died at the Ravensbrück concentration camp in December 1944.

Corrie eventually was able to leave the concentration camp due to a clerical error. While speaking in a church concerning God's forgiveness, she came face-to-face with one of the former Ravensbrück prison guards, who, not recognizing her, proceeded to ask her forgiveness for the atrocities he had committed. After a prayer, Corrie found the strength to forgive him that night. Forgiveness in action is amazing.

No one can go back and make a new beginning, but everyone can start from today and make a brand-new ending. What activates that is forgiveness.

Forgiveness is the key to personal peace. Forgiveness releases action and creates freedom. We all need to say the right thing after doing the wrong thing. Lawrence Sterne said, "Only the brave knows how to forgive. . . . A coward never forgave; it is not in his nature." Josiah Bailey reflected, "It is the truth that those who forgive most shall be most forgiven."

One of the secrets of a long and fruitful life is to forgive everybody everything every night before you go to bed. Peter Winter said, "It is manlike to punish but godlike to forgive." When you have a huge chip on your shoulder, it causes you to lose your balance. If you would quit nursing a grudge, it would die. You don't need a doctor to tell you it's better to remove a grudge than to nurse it.

Forgiveness is a funny thing. It warms the heart and cools the sting. It is far better to forgive and forget than to hate and remember. Josh Billings said, "There is no revenge so complete as forgiveness." Unforgiveness blocks blessings; forgiveness releases them.

Do you want to release the past and claim the future? Get ahold of what Paul Boese said: "Forgiveness does not change the past, but it does enlarge the future." Harry Fosdick commented, "No one can be wrong with man and right with God." You can be wrong in the middle of being right when you don't forgive someone. As a Yiddish proverb says, "Protest long enough that you are right, and you will be wrong."

The Bible says in Ephesians, "Let all bitterness, and wrath, and anger, and clamor, and evil-speaking, be put away from you, with all malice: and be ye kind one to another, tender-hearted, forgiving one another, even as God for Christ's sake hath forgiven you" (4:31–32 WBT). Ask yourself this question: "If God is willing to forgive, then who am I to hold out?"

> **The heaviest thing a person can carry is a grudge.**

How can you change someone's life for the better today?

A good way to judge a man is by what he says. A better way is by what he does. The best way is by what he gives. Elizabeth Bibesco said, "Blessed are those who give without remembering and take without forgetting." The big problem is not the haves and have-nots—it's the give-nots. The Lord loves a cheerful giver, and so does everyone else.

When author Brian Kluth's book *40-Day Spiritual Journey to a More Generous Life* became a bestseller, he was contacted by NBC. The TV reporter asked him, "Do you think God wants everyone to be rich?"

He replied, "No, I don't believe that."

"Well, what do you believe?"

"I believe that everyone needs to learn to become more generous with whatever God has given them," he said.

"Well, didn't your book becoming a bestseller make you rich?" the reporter asked.

"No," Brian responded, "it helped me become more generous!"

There are millions of people the world over who would gladly trade places with you and me. We should never lose the perspective of how blessed we are. How "rich" we are. And how much we have to give to others.

The secret to living is giving. Charles Spurgeon said, "Feel for others—in your pocket." An Indian proverb says, "Good people, like clouds, receive only to give away." In fact, the best generosity is that which is quick. When you give quickly it is like giving twice. R. Browne says, "Whatever God does in your life is not so you can keep it to yourself. He wants you to give to others." What He gets *to* you can get *through* you.

The Bible says, "It is more blessed to give than to receive" (Acts 20:35). Giving is always the thermometer of our love. Eleanor Roosevelt said, "When you cease to make a contribution, you begin to die." Getters don't find happiness. Givers do. When you live for another, it's the best way to live for yourself. John Wesley advised, "Make all you can, save all you can, give all you can." That's a good formula for a successful life.

The Swiss say, "A greedy person and a pauper are practically one and the same." When it comes to giving, some people stop at nothing. But greed always diminishes what has been gained. Mike Murdock says, "Giving is proof that you have conquered greed." When you give only after being asked, you have waited too long.

A lot of people are willing to give God the credit, but not too many are willing to give Him the cash. Don't cheat the Lord and call it savings. The trouble with too many people who give until it hurts is that they are so sensitive to pain.

If you have, give. If you lack, give. G. D. Boardman said, "The law of the harvest is to reap more than you sow." It is true: people who give always receive.

Henry Drummond said, "There is no happiness in having or in getting, but only in giving." The test of generosity is not necessarily how much you give but how much you have left. Henry David Thoreau said, "If you give money, spend yourself with it." The secret to living is giving.

What you give lives.

Are you having fun yet?

I have the privilege of being asked to speak at conferences, churches, and conventions. It is something that I've been doing nearly all my life.

One thing I love to do when I speak is to start my talk with a humorous story. This relaxes the audience and gives them permission to laugh at funny stories I may share later. And I believe it shows me being myself, which is probably the most important reason I do it.

Smiling is powerful. It's been proven that smiling boosts your immune system and relieves stress by releasing endorphins. Even babies are born with the ability to smile. From my view, God created us to have fun, laugh, and smile. Here's a story I love to tell at the beginning of many of my talks.

A long time ago, a young boy on his way to school in the morning would sneak into an old general store. He would go straight over to a large barrel that was full of molasses. He would dip his fingers in the molasses, eat it, and then run out the door before the owner of the store could catch him.

Well, as you might imagine, the owner of the store didn't like this at all, so he decided one day he was going to catch this boy and teach him a lesson.

So, like always, the young boy was heading to school and once again sneaked into the general store. But this time the owner of the store was hiding behind the door as the boy entered and headed straight over to the barrel full of molasses.

The boy was just about ready to dip his fingers in the molasses barrel when out from behind the door jumped the storekeeper. He grabbed the boy, picked him up, and was ready to thrust him headlong into the barrel full of molasses when he heard the boy say, "Lord, give me a tongue equal to this great opportunity."

As a speaker, I'm sure you can see why I like to use that story. And I guess as an author also I could say, "Lord, give me a pen/keyboard equal to this great opportunity."

The bottom line is, it's good to laugh. It can even improve your health. The Bible reminds us that "a merry heart doeth good like a medicine" (Prov. 17:22). No wonder so many people are dog-tired in the morning—it's probably because all they did the day before was growl.

There is a facelift you can perform yourself that is guaranteed to improve your appearance. It's called a smile.

A smile is a curve that helps us see things straight. It's a curve that you throw at someone else and always results in a hit. A smile goes a long way, but you're the one who must start it on its journey. Your world will look brighter from behind a smile. So smile often. Give your frown a rest.

Laughter is like changing a baby's diaper—it doesn't permanently solve any problems, but it makes things more acceptable for a while. The only medicine that needs no prescription, has no unpleasant taste, and costs no money is laughter. So cheer up. A dentist is the only person who is supposed to look down in the mouth.

Robert Frost said, "Happiness makes up in height for what it lacks in length." Abraham Lincoln said, "Most folks are about as happy as they make up their minds to be." The worst day you can have is the day you have not laughed.

The optimist laughs to forget. The pessimist forgets to laugh. You might as well laugh at yourself once in a while—everyone else does.

Henry Ward Beecher said, "A person without a sense of humor is like a wagon without springs. It's jolted by every pebble on the road." Take to heart the words of Moshe Waldoks: "A sense of humor can help you overlook the unattractive, tolerate the unpleasant, cope with the unexpected, and smile through the unbearable." Your day goes the way the corners of your mouth turn.

I believe that every time a man smiles, and even much more so when he laughs, he adds something to his life. Janet Lane said, "Of all the things you wear, your expression is the most important." A good laugh is the best medicine, whether you are sick or not.

"The world is like a mirror; frown at it, and it frowns at you. Smile and it smiles, too," Herbert Samuel said. Cheerfulness is contagious, but it seems like some folks have been vaccinated against the infection. The trouble with being a grouch is that you must make new friends every month. Every man who expects to receive happiness is obligated to give happiness. You have no right to consume it without producing it.

The wheels of progress are not turned by cranks. Tom Walsh said, "Every minute your mouth is turned down you lose 60 seconds of happiness." Paul Bourge wrote, "Unhappiness indicates wrong thinking, just as ill health indicates a bad regimen." It is almost impossible to smile on the outside without feeling better on the inside. If you can laugh at something, you can live with it.

He who laughs, lasts. (Robert Fulghum)

Are you choosing your story or someone else's?

What you see is not always what you get. Nothing is as it appears. So be careful when you compare what you *think* is going on in another person's life with what you *know* is going on in your life.

Nothing is more telling in this regard than the photos we present of ourselves. I've always said that a good picture is one that doesn't really look like you.

Have you noticed people rarely look like their picture? I know I've been guilty of this. I left my thirty-something picture on my book cover for nearly twenty years. People who were sent to pick me up at the airport have walked right past me with my book in their hand, looking for the man on the cover!

I guess we all want to use the best picture, no matter when it was taken, because it looks good today. And it looks even better as the years progress.

Several years ago, I met with a friend I have known for over ten years. He said to me, "John, I see all the great things that God has done in your life and how He has caused you to increase in every way. But as I began to look at *your* life, I became full of doubt as to what God was doing in *my* life. I saw what He had done in yours, and I began to doubt that God was really working in mine, because I haven't had the same success."

I replied, "Well, if it's true that you feel bad because God has been good to me, then would it be true that you would feel better if I'd had terrible failures and had been doing much worse over the past several years?"

He gave me a quizzical look and responded, "No, that would not be true."

"Well, if it's true for one, it's true for the other," I said. "Really, it shows how inaccurate your thinking is. What happens in my life has nothing to do with what God is doing in your life."

You will find that God rarely uses people whose main concern is what others are thinking. I believe that judging others is a major waste of time. Judgment halts progress and always inhibits forward motion.

Some are inclined to measure their achievement by what others have *not* done. Never determine your success by that. You are either a thermometer or a thermostat. You register either someone else's temperature or your own. Pat Riley said, "Don't let other people tell you what you want." No one can build a personal destiny upon the faith or experience of another person. "Don't take anybody else's definition of success as your own," Jacqueline Briskin advised.

Your faults will never vanish by you calling attention to the faults of others. Many people have the mistaken idea that they can make themselves great by showing how small someone else is. Instead of letting their own light shine, some people spend their time trying to put out the lights of others. What a waste!

If you think you're doing better than the average person, *you're* an average person. Why would you want to compare yourself with someone average? Too many people seem to know how to live everybody's life but their own. We need to stop comparing ourselves to others.

> **Don't measure your success by what others have or haven't done.**

Question 21

What gives you goose bumps?

Nothing great happens without enthusiasm.

My wife, Linda, and I both remember well our first "real" date. I borrowed a car from her friend, and we went on a double date to a popular pizza place near the university we were attending. From the first few minutes together, we were having a great time. We talked like we had known each other for years. We were laughing, intently listening to each other, and just having an overall fun date. The other couple, however, was not doing so well. Kind of like two statues looking at each other.

I was feeling enthusiastic and excited about Linda, and later she told me she felt the same way about me. As our time at the pizza place ended and we headed back to campus, the car began to sputter and stopped. It had run out of gas. (No, I didn't do this on purpose.) The owner of the car had told me that the gas gauge was broken but he thought there was plenty of gas for us. He clearly miscalculated.

We began to walk back to school, all four of us. The school we attended had a curfew for the young ladies but not for the men. I know this seems unfair today, but that's the way it was back then.

As we walked, Linda got more and more nervous, and it was apparent she was going to miss curfew. I'm sure she'd never been in this kind of trouble before, but we were so thrilled with our time together that it seemed to have been well worth it.

Yes, she was late, and yes, the school even punished her by not allowing her to go out at all the next weekend. What would've been a mortal sin to her became not such a big deal because something good was starting between us. We were both excited about what the future held.

Excitement and enthusiasm are the only way to start and build any worthwhile thing in your life. Relationships, businesses, ministries, personal relationships — are all best served on a platter of enthusiasm and excitement.

"Think excitement, talk excitement, act out excitement, and you are bound to become an excited person. Life will take on a new zest, deeper interest and greater meaning. You can talk, think and act yourself into dullness or into monotony or into unhappiness. By the same process you can build up inspiration, excitement and surging depth of joy," Norman Vincent Peale said. You can succeed at almost anything for which you have limitless enthusiasm. Enthusiasm moves the world.

According to Henry Chester, "Enthusiasm is nothing more or less than faith in action." Your enthusiasm reflects your reserves, your unexploited resources, and perhaps your future. One real difference between people is their level of enthusiasm. Winston Churchill said, "Success is going from failure to failure without loss of enthusiasm." You will never rise to great truths and heights without joy and enthusiasm.

"No one keeps up his enthusiasm automatically," Papyrus said. It must be nourished with new actions, new aspirations, new efforts, and new vision. It's your own fault if your enthusiasm is gone. You have failed to feed it. Helen Keller said, "Optimism is the faith that leads to achievement. Nothing can be done without hope or confidence."

It isn't our position but our disposition that makes us happy. Remember, some people freeze in the winter; others ski. A positive attitude always creates positive results. Attitude is a little thing that makes a big difference. Depression, gloom, pessimism, despair, discouragement, and fear slay more human beings than all illnesses combined.

You can't deliver the goods if your heart is heavier than the load. "We act as though comfort and luxury were the chief requirements of life, when all that we need to make us really happy is something to be enthusiastic about," Charles Kingsley said. Some people count their blessings, but most think their blessings don't count.

There is a direct correlation between our passion and our potential. You can be the light of the world, but the switch must be turned on. Being positive is essential to achievement and the foundation of true progress. If you live a life of negativity, you will find yourself seasick during the entire voyage. The person who is negative is half defeated before even beginning.

I agree with Winston Churchill when he said, "I am an optimist. It does not seem too much use being anything else." Have you ever noticed that no matter how many worries a pessimist has, they always have room for one more? Remember the Chinese proverb: "It is better to light a candle than to curse the darkness." As Paul Williams said in *Das Energi*, "Vote with your life; vote yes!"

The world belongs to the enthusiastic.

Question 22

Have you survived the worst thing that's happened to you?

Everyone faces obstacles. Sometimes we're the cause of the obstacles. Sometimes it's other people. Sometimes it's just plain circumstances or timing. One thing is for certain—how we respond to obstacles makes all the difference.

As a big brother with two younger sisters, I admit, I became an obstacle to them many times. I did many "big brother" kinds of things. If my sister was in the bathroom in the house we grew up in, I would try to find a spider I could nudge underneath the door, listening with delight as her screams grew louder the closer the spider approached.

Our phone, which had a long extension cord, was used to create more havoc when friends or boys would call. I would answer and say, "Just a minute, she's in the bathroom." I'd stretch the phone to the nearby bathroom, flush the toilet with the phone just above the bowl, then give the call to one of my sisters. It also wasn't uncommon for me to pay certain unpopular boys to ring our doorbell and ask for either of my sisters.

Yes, I was an obstacle. Fortunately, both my sisters ended up unharmed and are doing quite well despite their prankster big brother.

Obstacles come, but no obstacle leaves you the way it finds you. You'll always be better or you'll be worse—the decision is up to you.

"Times of general calamity and confusion have been productive of the greatest minds. The purest ore is produced from the hottest furnace, and the brightest thunderbolt is elicited from the darkest storm," Charles Colton said. The door to opportunity swings on the hinges of opposition. Problems are the price of progress. The obstacles of life are intended to make us better, not bitter.

Obstacles are merely a call to strengthen, not quit, your resolve to achieve worthwhile goals. Bob Harrison said, "Between you and anything significant will be giants in your path." Oral Roberts reflected, "You cannot bring about renewal or change without confrontation." The truth is, if you like things easy, you will have difficulties. If you like problems, you will succeed.

If you have a dream without aggravations, you don't have a dream. Have the attitude of Louisa May Alcott: "I am not afraid of storms for I am learning how to sail my ship." Samuel Lover said, "Circumstances are the rulers of the weak; but they are the instruments of the wise." The Chinese have a proverb that says, "The gem cannot be polished without friction, nor man perfected without trials." It seems that great trials are the necessary preparation for greatness.

For every obstacle you face, I believe God has provided a Scripture as your answer. Mike Murdock said, "If God 'cushioned' your every blow, you would never learn to grow." Don't let your problems take the lead. Instead, you take the lead. The problem you face is simply an opportunity for you to do your best. Conflict is good when you know how to move with God.

What attitude do we need to have toward difficulties? William Boetcker said, "The difficulties and struggles of today are but the best price we must pay for the accomplishments and victories of tomorrow." Lou Holtz reflected, "Adversity is another way to measure the greatness of individuals. I never had a crisis that didn't make me stronger."

You will find that when you encounter obstacles, you will discover things about yourself that you never knew. Challenges make you stretch—they make you go beyond the norm. Martin Luther King Jr. said, "The ultimate measure of man is not where he stands in moments of comfort and convenience, but where he stands at times of challenge and controversy." Turning an obstacle to your advantage is the first necessary step toward victory.

God promises a safe landing, but not necessarily a calm voyage. Life is as uncertain as a grapefruit's squirt. Consider what Sydney Harris said: "When I hear somebody say, 'Life is hard,' I am always tempted to ask, 'Compared to what?'"

We might as well face our problems. We can't run fast enough or far enough to get away from them all. Rather, we should have the attitude of Stan Musial, the Hall of Fame baseball player. Commenting on how to handle a spitball, he said, "I'll just hit the dry side of the ball." Charles Kettering said, "No one would have crossed the ocean if he could have gotten off the ship in the storm." The breakfast of champions is not cereal; it's obstacles.

Adversity has advantages.

Question 23

Is it true?

An atheist brought a discrimination case to court over the upcoming Easter and Passover holy days. The argument was that it was unfair that atheists had no such recognized days.

After the judge listened to the passionate presentation, he banged his gavel, declaring, "Case dismissed!"

The atheist's lawyer immediately stood, objecting to the ruling. "Your Honor, how can you possibly dismiss this case? The Christians have Christmas, Easter, and others. The Jews have Passover, Yom Kippur, and Hanukkah. Yet my client and all other atheists have no such holiday."

The judge leaned forward in his chair, saying, "But you do. Your client, Counsel, is woefully ignorant. The calendar says April 1st is April Fools' Day. Psalm 14:1 states, 'The fool says in his heart, "There is no God."' Thus, it is the opinion of this court that if your client says there is no God, then he is a fool. Therefore, April 1st is his day. Court is adjourned."

That's telling the truth!

There is no limit to the height a man can attain by remaining on the level. Honesty is still the best policy. However, today there are fewer policyholders than there used to be. Georges Braque said, "Truth exists, only falsehood has to be invented." Cervantes said, "Truth will rise above falsehood as oil above water."

You can't stretch the truth without making your story look pretty thin. And when you do stretch the truth, it will snap back at you. Truth will win every argument if you stick with it long enough. Though it may not be popular, it is always right. The fact that nobody wants to believe something doesn't keep it from being true.

Two half-truths do not necessarily constitute the whole truth. In fact, beware of half-truths. You may have gotten hold of the wrong half. You will find that a lie has no legs; it must be supported by other lies. The truth is one thing for which there are no known substitutes. There is no acceptable substitute for honesty, and there is no valid excuse for dishonesty.

Nothing shows dirt like a white lie. At times a fib starts out as a little white lie, but it usually ends up as a double feature in Technicolor. It may appear to you that a lie will take care of the present, but it actually has no future.

The only way to truly be free is to be a person of truth. The book of John asserts, "You shall know the truth, and the truth shall make you free" (8:32 NKJV). Truth is strong and it will prevail. The truth outlives a lie.

A shady person never produces a bright life. Herbert Casson said, "Show me a liar and I will show you a thief." A liar will not be believed even though he tells the truth. George Bernard Shaw said, "The liar's punishment is not in the least that he is not believed, but that he cannot believe anyone else." Liars have no true friends.

"If you lie and then tell the truth, the truth will be considered a lie," a Sumerian proverb says. An honest man alters his ideas to fit the truth, and a dishonest man alters the truth to fit his ideas. There are no degrees of honesty.

The Bible says, "Do not let kindness and truth leave you; bind them around your neck, write them on the tablet of your heart" (Prov. 3:3 NASB). Margaret Lee Runbeck said, "There is no power on earth more formidable than the truth." And consider what Pearl Buck said: "The truth is always exciting. Speak it, then. Life is dull without it."

White lies leave black marks.

Question 24

What one thing do you need to do next?

There is nothing quite like taking the right action at the right time to do what you know you should do.

While I was head of the publishing company in Florida, I was also the main person responsible for all author acquisitions. I would make decisions about which authors we would publish and which we wouldn't, those we would pursue and those we would stay away from.

From the very start, I've had this publishing philosophy: I want to publish books from authors on subjects that are getting fruit. In other words, results. From my viewpoint, the best books are those that take what God is doing through a person and put that content into print. Unfortunately, today nearly all book publishing decisions are made based on previous book-selling history and size of platform. But that is another subject.

I'll never forget one publishing decision that impacted more than one million people. Let me share that story with you.

I had become friends with a young, enthusiastic minister named John Bevere. John and I were not only friends and fellow ministers but also golfing buddies. It was common on many of our golf outings for us to talk about all the good things that were happening in his ministry and in my efforts with the publishing company.

At work, I had sensed in my heart that there was a need for a book about how to respond to being offended. I'd seen so many people trapped by this and knew that a book on the subject would get a big response and help a lot of people.

I took notice when John began to share with me how the Lord had laid it on his heart to begin to preach about the subject of overcoming offenses. The more I listened to John, the more I became convinced that God was using him to help people in this area. There was an incredible response and fruit, and John was very passionate about the subject.

At that time, John had self-published a couple books, and his ministry was small but growing. Candidly, his current platform and previous bookselling history didn't rise to the level of a publishing house our size. But I was sure in my heart that he was the man to write the book on the subject.

I decided I would talk with the owner of the publishing company, my boss, about releasing a book with John. My boss was a very astute businessman. I knew that when I talked with him about this book, I would have to be able to defend the financial reasons for doing it.

As I discussed the book, it became apparent that he didn't share the same view as me, but he did say, "You've made a lot of money for me, so we can do this book. But if it fails, it'll be on you."

I responded immediately, "That's fine with me. I want to do the book."

A few days later, John and I scheduled a golf outing. I drove up to the country club of Mount Dora, turned to John, and said, "I want to publish a book with you on overcoming offenses. I even have the title for you. It's from my book *You're Born an Original—Don't Die a Copy*. In my book, I say that being offended is the bait of Satan to get you out of the will of God. I think you should call this book *The Bait of Satan*."

We published that book, and it became our number one bestseller that year. It has now sold over one million copies worldwide and has been published in many languages. It has helped many, many people.

Let me ask you the age-old question: Are you waiting on God, or is He waiting on you? I believe the clear majority of the time, He is waiting on us. Is God your hope or your excuse? I'm convinced He wants us to take the initiative to live our life on the offensive. William Menninger said, "The amount of satisfaction you get from life depends largely on your own ingenuity, self-sufficiency, and resourcefulness. People who wait around for life to supply their satisfaction usually find boredom instead."

Elbert Hubbard remarked, "Parties who want milk should not seat themselves on a stool in the middle of the field in hope that the cow will back up to them." The door of opportunity won't open unless you push.

Being on the defensive has never produced ultimate victory. I believe that God helps the courageous. Do like Sara Teasdale said: "I make the most of all that comes and the least of all that goes."

E. M. Bounds said, "There is neither encouragement nor room in Bible religion for feeble desires, listless efforts, lazy attitudes; all must be strenuous, urgent, ardent. Flamed desires, impassioned, unwary insistence delights heaven. God would have His children incorrigibly in earnest and persistently bold in their efforts." When you are bold, His mighty powers will come to your aid.

Helen Keller advised, "Never bend your head. Hold it high. Look the world straight in the eye." If you want success, you must seize your own opportunities as you go. I agree with Jonathan Winters: "I couldn't wait for success — so I went ahead without it." Lillian Hellman said, "It is best to act with confidence, no matter how little right you have to it." It is always a bumpy, uphill road that leads to heights of greatness.

George Adams said, "In this life we only get those things for which we hunt, for which we strive and for which we are willing to sacrifice." Don't just face opportunities and problems; attack them. Consider what B. C. Forbes said: "Mediocre men wait for opportunities to come to them. Strong, able, alert men go after opportunity."

> **Don't sit back and take what comes.
> Go after what you want.**

What have you started that you need to finish?

Never give up on what you know God wants you to do. No matter what. As Winston Churchill said, "Never give up on something that you can't go a day without thinking about."

As someone once said, "God has a purpose for your pain, a reason for your struggles, and a gift for your faithfulness. Don't give up." You can't beat a person who doesn't quit.

Nothing great comes easily. The fact is, you don't know what's going to happen next. Miracles happen every day. Things can happen quickly.

I'm blessed to have lived long enough to look back gratefully. Although we don't always understand everything that happens to us, many times God does reveal why we go through what we do. Everything that has happened in your life prepares you for what is to come.

There is something valuable in even our most difficult struggles.

Was it not Alfred Russel Wallace who tried to help an emperor-moth, and only harmed it by his ill-considered ministry? He came upon the creature beating its wings and struggling wildly to force its passage through the narrow neck of its cocoon. He admired its fine proportions, eight inches from the tip of one wing to the tip of the other, and thought it a pity that so handsome a creature should be subjected to so severe an ordeal. He therefore took out his lancet and slit the cocoon. The moth came out at once; but its glorious colours never developed. The soaring wings never expanded. The indescribable hues and tints and shades that should have adorned them never appeared. The moth crept moodily about; drooped perceptibly; and presently died. The furious struggle with the cocoon was Nature's wise way of developing the splendid wings and of sending the vital fluids pulsing through the frame until every particle blushed with their beauty. The naturalist had saved the little creature from the struggle, but had unintentionally ruined and slain it in the process.

F. W. Boreham

Do you want to accomplish something in life? Be like the stone cutter. Jacob Riis said, "Look at the stone cutter hammering away at the rock, perhaps 100 times without as much as a crack showing in it. Yet at the 101st blow it will split in two and I know it was not the last blow that did it, but all that had gone before." Whatever you want to accomplish in life will require persistence.

All things come to those who go after them. Perseverance is the result of a strong will. Stubbornness is the result of a strong won't. Montesquieu said, "Success often depends on knowing how long it will take to succeed." The secret of success: never let down and never let up. Many times, success consists of hanging on one minute longer.

Calvin Coolidge said, "'Press on' has solved and always will solve the problems of the human race." You will find that persistent people always have this attitude: they never lose the game; they just run out of time.

All spiritual progress is like an unfolding vegetable bud. You first have a leading, then peace, then conviction, as the plant has root, bud, and fruit. Comte de Buffon said, "Never think that God's delays are God's denials. Hold on; hold fast; hold out. Patience is genius."

Joel Hawes said, "You may be whatever you resolve to be. Determine to be something in the world and you will be something. 'I cannot' never accomplished anything; 'I will try' has wrought wonders." Herbert Kaufman commented, "Spurts don't count. The final score makes no mention of a splendid start if the finish proves that you were an 'also ran.'" Keep in mind the words of Hamilton Holt: "Nothing worthwhile comes easily. Half effort does not produce half results. It produces no results. Work, continuous work and hard work, is the only way to accomplish results that last."

Persistence prevails when all else fails. The truth is that persistence is a bitter plant, but it has sweet fruit. Joseph Ross said, "It takes time to succeed because success is merely the natural reward of taking time to do anything well." Ecclesiastes 7:8 declares, "Better is the end of a thing than the beginning thereof: and the patient in spirit is better than the proud in spirit." Victory always comes to the most persevering.

Ralph Waldo Emerson said, "The great majority of men are bundles of beginnings." I agree with Charles Kettering when he said, "Keep on going and the chances are you will stumble on something, perhaps when you are least expecting it." No one finds life worth living; one must make it worth living. Persistence is the quality that is most needed when it is exhausted. Often *genius* is just another way of spelling *persistence*.

To finish first, you must first finish. (Rick Mears)

Do you scare yourself?

Dreams bring clarity and a view of your future.

In the Bering Strait, two small islands lie about two miles apart. Between them is the United States–Russia boundary, which coincides with the international date line. These islands are known as Big Diomede, which belongs to Russia, and Little Diomede, which belongs to the United States. Russia has an important weather station on their island, and Little Diomede Island is a part of Alaska inhabited by Chukchi people.

This location creates an interesting situation. If you are standing on the shore of Little Diomede looking over at Big Diomede, not only are you looking over into another country, but you are looking over into another time. And on a clear day, you can see tomorrow.

Look at your future from a position of faith. By doing that you can believe and see your tomorrows before they happen. This pleases God, for "without faith it is impossible to please him" (Heb. 11:6).

Don't do anything that doesn't require faith. G. C. Lichtenberg said, "Never undertake anything for which you wouldn't have the courage to ask the blessings of heaven." Psalm 56:9 reads, "When I cry unto thee, then shall mine enemies turn back: this I know; for God is for me." Accept and acknowledge only those thoughts that contribute to your success, that line up with God's Word and His will for your life.

Wayne Gretzky is, arguably, the greatest hockey player in history. Asked about his secret for continuing to lead the National Hockey League in goals year after year, Gretzky replied, "I skate to where the puck is going to be, not where it has been." Dare to go farther than you can see. "Seek not to understand that thou mayest believe, but believe that thou mayest understand," Saint Augustine said.

Too many people expect little from God, ask little, and therefore receive little and are content with little. Sherwood Eddy said, "Faith is not trying to believe something regardless of the evidence; faith is daring to do something regardless of the consequences." I sincerely believe that we would accomplish many more things if we did not so automatically view them as impossible.

God gave man an upright countenance to survey the heavens and look upward toward him. Don't ever say that conditions are not right. This will always limit God. If you wait for conditions to be exactly right, you will never obey God. The Bible says in the book of Isaiah, "If you are willing and obedient, you will eat the good things of the land" (1:19 NIV).

Those who dare, do; those who dare not, do not. Isak Dinesen said, "God made the world round so we would never be able to see too far down the road." The person who dares for nothing need hope for nothing. You have reached stagnation when all you ever exercise is caution. Sometimes you must press ahead despite the pounding fear in your head that says, "Turn back."

If God is kept outside, something must be wrong inside. He will never allow anything to confront you that you and He together can't handle. Mary Lyon said it best: "Trust in God—and do something."

God said, "Come to the edge."
We said, "It's too high."
"Come to the edge."
We said, "We might fall."
"Come to the edge," God said.
And we came.
And He nudged us.
And we flew.

> **Don't wait for all the lights to be green before you leave the house.** (Jim Stovall)

Question 27

What are you putting off today that you put off yesterday?

An incident from the American Revolution illustrates what tragedy can result from procrastination.

It is reported that Colonel Johann Rall, commander of the British troops at Trenton, New Jersey, was playing cards when a courier brought an urgent message stating that General George Washington was crossing the Delaware River. Rall put the letter in his pocket and didn't bother to read it until the game was finished.

Then, realizing the seriousness of the situation, he hurriedly tried to rally his men to meet the coming attack, but his procrastination was his undoing. He and many of his men were killed, and the rest of the regiment was captured. Nolbert Quayle said, "Only a few minutes' delay cost him his life, his honor, and the liberty of his soldiers. Earth's history is strewn with the wrecks of half-finished plans and unexecuted resolutions. 'Tomorrow' is the excuse of the lazy and the refuge of the incompetent."

Ask yourself, "If I don't take action now, what will this ultimately cost me?" When a procrastinator has finally made up his mind, the opportunity has always passed by.

What you put off until tomorrow, you'll probably put off tomorrow too. Success comes to the man who does today what others were thinking of doing tomorrow. The lazier a man is, the more he is going to do tomorrow. "All problems become smaller if you don't dodge them, but confront them. Touch a thistle timidly, and it pricks you; grasp it boldly, and its spines crumble," William Halsey said.

Wasting time wastes your life. Cervantes pondered, "By the street of By and By, one arrives at the house of Never." A lazy person doesn't go through life—he's pushed through it. "The wise man does at once what the fool does finally," Baltasar Gracián said. "Someday" is not a day of the week. Doing nothing is the most tiresome job in the world. When you won't start, your difficulties won't stop. Tackle any difficulty now—the longer you wait, the bigger it grows. Procrastinators never have small problems because they always wait until their problems grow up.

In the game of life, nothing is less important than the score at halftime. "The tragedy of life is not that man loses, but that he almost wins," Heywood Broun said. Some people wait so long, the future is gone before they get there.

Most people who sit around waiting for their ship to come in often find it is hardship. The thing that comes to a man who waits seldom turns out to be the thing he's waited for. The hardest work in the world is that which should have been done yesterday. Hard work is usually an accumulation of easy things that should have been done last week.

Sir Josiah Stamp said, "It is easy to dodge our responsibilities, but we cannot dodge the consequences of dodging our responsibilities." William James reflected, "Nothing is so fatiguing as the eternal hanging on of an uncompleted task." People who delay action until all factors are perfect do nothing. Jimmy Lyons said, "Tomorrow is the only day in the year that appeals to a lazy man."

According to E. R. Collcord, "A man with nothing to do does far more strenuous 'labor' than any other form of work. But my greatest pity is for the man who dodges a job he knows he should do. He is a shirker, and boy! What punishment he takes . . . from himself."

> **Procrastination is the fertilizer that makes difficulties grow.**

Is the juice worth the squeeze?

Jesus taught we should strive to bear good fruit with our lives. So our purpose, work, and efforts should result in "juice" worth the "squeeze" of the life we choose.

It was a beautiful day in Tulsa, Oklahoma. I was driving my car, minding my own business, heading to an appointment west of the city. To this day, I can tell you exactly where I was when I heard this in my heart: *John, there are three things I want you to do in your life and ministry. First, you will be a divine connection for people. Second, you will be able to see the gifts and callings in people, and what you do will stir those up in them. Third, you will be able to discern the truth from a lie.*

And that is what I did . . . and have tried to do from that day forward. Not only was God giving me some understanding of what my gifts and strengths were, He was also helping me understand my purpose. I knew that everything I did from that day forward would somehow involve those three areas.

Are you stumbling toward an uncertain future? You can predict your future by the awareness you have of your purpose. Too many people know what they are running from, but not what they are running to. First concentrate on finding your purpose, then concentrate on fulfilling it. Having a powerful *why* will provide you with the necessary *how*. Purpose, not money, is your real asset.

Take care of your purpose and the end will take care of itself. When you base your life on principle, 99 percent of your decisions are already made. Purpose does what it must; talent does what it can. Considering an action? Listen to Marcus Aurelius: "Without a purpose nothing should be done." Robert Byrne said, "The purpose of life is a life of purpose."

As you reach for your destiny, it will be like a magnet that pulls you, not like a brass ring that only goes around once. Destiny draws.

John Foster said, "It is a poor disgraceful thing not to be able to reply, with some degree of certainty, to the simple questions, 'What will you be? What will you do?'" Dr. Charles Garfield noted, "Top performers are committed to a compelling mission. It is very clear that they care deeply about what they do and their efforts, energies and enthusiasms are traceable back to that particular mission." You're not truly free until you've been made captive by your supreme mission in life.

Don't just pray that God will do this or that; rather, pray that God will make His purpose known to you. William Cowper said, "The only true happiness comes from squandering ourselves for a purpose."

As individuals go their right way, destiny accompanies them. Don't part company with your destiny. It is an anchor in the storm. A purposeless life is an early death. Psalm 138:8 reads, "The LORD will fulfill his purpose for me; your steadfast love, O LORD, endures forever" (ESV).

Rick Renner commented, "The only thing that will keep you from the will of God is if you look at yourself and say, 'I'm not so much among so many.'" You can't do anything about the length of your life, but you can do something about its width and depth. What you believe is the force that determines what you accomplish or fail to accomplish in life.

The average person's life consists of twenty years of parents asking where he or she is going, forty years of a spouse asking the same question, and at the end of life, mourners wondering the same thing. Martin Luther King Jr. said, "If a man hasn't discovered something that he will die for, he isn't fit to live." Abandon yourself to destiny.

> **There is something for you to start that is ordained for you to finish.** (Myles Monroe)

What would you do today if there were no tomorrow?

I am standing upon the seashore. A ship at my side spreads her white sails to the morning breeze and starts for the blue ocean. She is an object of beauty and strength, and I stand and watch until at last she hangs like a speck of white cloud, just where the sea and sky come down to mingle with each other. Then someone at my side says, "There she goes!"

Gone where? Gone from my sight . . . that is all. She is just as large in mast and hull and spar as she was when she left my side and just as able to bear her load of living freight to the place of destination. Her diminished size is in me, not in her. And just at the moment when someone at my side says, "There she goes!" there are other eyes watching her coming and other voices ready to take up the glad shout, "Here she comes!"

Henry Van Dyke

Seize the moment! "Miracles are coming by you or to you every day," Oral Roberts said. Today was once the future from which you expected so much in the past. Horatio Dresser said, "The ideal never comes. Today is ideal for him who makes it so." Live for today. Don't let what you have within your grasp today be missed entirely because only the future intrigued you and the past disheartened you.

Doing the best at this moment puts you in the best place for the next moment. When can you live if not now? All the flowers of tomorrow are in the seeds of today. Seneca said, "Begin at once to live." Ellen Metcalf remarked, "There are many people who are at the right place at the right time but don't know it." It is okay to take time to plan, but when the time of action has arrived, stop thinking and go for it!

The book of Psalms says, "Teach us to number our days, that we may apply our hearts unto wisdom" (90:12). Maria Edgeworth said, "There is no moment like the present. The man who will not execute his resolutions when they are fresh on him can have no hope from them afterwards; for they will be dissipated, lost, and perished in the hurry and scurry of the world, or sunk in the slough of indolence."

John Burroughs said, "The lesson which life repeats and constantly enforces is, 'Look under foot.' You are always nearer the divine and the true sources of your power than you think. . . . The great opportunity is where you are. Do not despise your own place and hour." The most important thing in our lives is what we are doing now.

Know the real value of today. Jonathan Swift said, "May you live all the days of your life." The future that you long and dream for begins today. Ralph Waldo Emerson advised, "Write it on your heart that every day is the best day of the year."

The regrets that most people experience in life come from failing to act when having an opportunity. Albert Dunning said, "Great opportunities come to all, but many do not know that they have met them. The only preparation to take advantage of them is . . . to watch what each day brings."

As Martialis said, "Tomorrow's life is too late; live today." Wayne Dyer observed, "Now is all we have. Everything that has ever happened, anything that is ever going to happen to you, is just a thought." Today, well lived, will prepare you for both the opportunities and the obstacles of tomorrow.

Few know when to rise to the occasion. Most only know when to sit down. Many spend too much time dreaming of the future, never realizing that a little of it arrives every day. I agree with Ruth Schabaker when she said, "Every day comes bearing its own gifts. Untie the ribbons."

> **Noah didn't wait for his ship to come in—he built one.**

Question 30

Whom did you love today?

We all need each other. There will be times when someone else needs exactly what you have.

Jimmy Durante was a singer, comedian, and actor during the early and middle part of the twentieth century. During World War II, Ed Sullivan asked him to entertain a group of soldiers who had just gotten back from the war and were temporarily staying on Ellis Island. Jimmy said he would, but he only had time for a short performance because he had to catch a ferry in time to do his radio show back in New York.

But when Jimmy got on stage, something interesting happened. He went through a short monologue and then stayed. The applause grew louder and louder, and he kept performing. Soon, he had been on stage fifteen, twenty, then thirty minutes.

Finally, he took a last bow and left the stage. Backstage someone stopped him and said, "I thought you had to go after a few minutes. What happened?"

Jimmy answered, "I did have to go, but I can show you the reason I stayed. You can see for yourself if you'll look down on the front row."

In the front row were two men, each of whom had lost an arm in the war. One had lost his right arm, the other his left. Together, they could clap, and that's exactly what they were doing, loudly and cheerfully.

Everyone benefits when we help each other.

A wonderful thing a person can do for their heavenly Father is to be kind to His children. Serving others is one of life's most awesome privileges. Albert Schweitzer said, "The only ones among you who will really be happy are those who will have sought and found how to serve."

Pierre de Chardin commented, "The most satisfying thing in life is to have been able to give a large part of one's self to others." Proverbs declares, "He who despises his neighbor sins; but he who has mercy on the poor, happy is he" (14:21 NKJV). Follow the counsel of Karl Reiland: "In about the same degree as you are helpful you will be happy."

Hunt for the good points in people. Remember that they must do the same in your case. Then do something to help them. If you want to get ahead, be a bridge, not a wall. Love others more than they deserve. Each human being presents us with an opportunity to serve. Everybody needs help from somebody.

John Andrew Holmes said, "The entire population of the universe, with one trifling exception, is composed of others." Too often we expect everyone else to practice the Golden Rule. The Golden Rule may be old, but it hasn't been used enough to show any signs of wear. We make a first-class mistake if we treat others as second-class people.

You can't help others without helping yourself. Kindness is one of the most difficult things to give away since it usually comes back to you. The person who sows seeds of kindness enjoys a perpetual harvest. I agree with Henry Drummond when he said, "I wonder why it is that we are not kinder to each other.... How much the world needs it! How easily it is done!"

Do you want to get along better with others? Be a little kinder than necessary. A good way to forget your own troubles is to help others out of theirs. When you share, you do not lessen; you increase your life.

Theodore Spear said, "You can never expect too much of yourself in the matter of giving yourself to others." The taller bamboo grows, the lower it bends. Martin Luther King Jr. said, "Everybody can be great . . . because anybody can serve." When you walk in the fruit of the Spirit, others can taste of it. Harry Fosdick commented, "One of the most amazing things ever said is Jesus' statement, 'He that is greatest among you shall be your servant.' None have one chance in a billion of being thought of as really great a century after they're gone except those who have been servants of all."

> Have you had a kindness shown?
> Pass it on.
> 'Twas not given for thee alone,
> Pass it on.
> Let it travel down the years,
> Let it wipe another's tears;
> Till in heaven the deed appears,
> Pass it on.
>
> Henry Burton

The Golden Rule is of no use whatsoever unless you realize that it is your move. (Dr. Frank Crane)

Question 31

What's the first small step you can take now to get moving in the right direction?

Small steps make a big difference.

A big-game hunter in India sighted a large Bengal tiger. Since the animal was only a short distance away, the hunter took a quick shot and missed. The tiger leaped toward the hunter, and fortunately, the animal jumped over him and he escaped.

The relieved hunter returned to camp and was concerned about his poor aim. So the next morning he went behind the camp to practice shooting at short range. As he was practicing, he heard rustling in the bushes nearby. He looked, and there was the same tiger, practicing short leaps.

Sometimes it is not the big goal that makes a difference but the short leaps that are significant. There are short leaps we can all use to improve our life and move us in the right direction.

Dale Carnegie said, "Don't be afraid to give your best to what seemingly are small jobs. Every time you conquer one it makes you that much stronger. If you do the little jobs well, the big ones will tend to take care of themselves." Your future comes one hour at a time. Thomas Huxley observed, "The rung of a ladder was never meant to rest upon, but only to hold a man's foot long enough to enable a man to put the other somewhat higher."

Never be discouraged when you make progress, no matter how slow. Only be wary of standing still. A success is a person who does what they can with what they have, where they are, no matter how small it is. Helen Keller said, "I long to accomplish a great and noble task, but it is my chief duty to accomplish small tasks as if they were great and noble."

All glory comes from daring to take small steps. After being faithful in small steps, you'll look back and say, "I'm still not where I want to be, but I'm not where I was." Julia Carney said, "Little drops of water, little grains of sand, make the mighty ocean and the pleasant land." Author Louis L'Amour wrote, "Victory is won not in miles but in inches. Win a little now, hold your ground, and later, win a lot more." God often gives us a little to see what we will do with a lot.

"Nobody made a greater mistake than he who did nothing because he could only do a little," Edmund Burke observed. Small deeds done are better than great deeds planned. I believe that God cares just as much about the small things in your life as the big things. Why? Because He knows if you are faithful in the small things, the big things will take care of themselves.

The prize of doing one duty is the opportunity to do another. Robert Smith said, "Most of the critical things in life, which become the starting points of human destiny, are little things." Do little things now, and big things will come to you, asking to be done.

One thing is for sure: what isn't tried won't work. The most important thing is to begin even though the first step is the hardest. I agree with Vince Lombardi: "Inches make champions." Take one small step right now. Don't ignore the small things. It's the little things that count: sometimes a safety pin carries more responsibility than a bank president.

David Storey remarked, "Have confidence that if you have done a *little* thing well, you could do a *bigger* thing well too." Consider what Pat Robertson said: "Despise not the day of small beginnings, because you can make all your mistakes anonymously." Value the little things. One day you may look back and realize they were the big things. As Dante said, "From a little spark may burst a mighty flame." Remember this on your way up: the biggest dog was once a pup.

Small steps—what a big idea!

Question 32

What's already in your hand?

Everyone has something they're good at.

Bugs Bunny was shopping at the supermarket, and a sales assistant said to him, "If you can tell me what 19,866 times 10,543 is, we'll give you free carrots for life."

Immediately, Bugs responded, "209,447,238."

The sales assistant was astonished and asked, "How on earth did you do that?"

Bugs replied, "If there's one thing rabbits are good at, it's multiplying."

Start with what you have, not with what you don't have. Pay attention to what you do well and easily.

Opportunity is always where you are, never where you were. To get anywhere you must launch out for somewhere or you will get nowhere. Hamilton Mabie said, "The question for each man to settle is not what he would do if he had the means, time, influence and education advantages, but what he will do with the things he has." God will always give us an ability to create what we need from something that is already here.

Each person tends to underrate or overrate that which they do not possess. E. W. Howe said, "People are always neglecting something they can do in trying to do something they can't do." I agree with Teddy Roosevelt when he said, "Do what you can, with what you have, where you are." The only way to learn anything thoroughly is by starting at the bottom (except when learning how to swim). To be successful, do what you can.

Ken Keyes Jr. said, "To be upset over what you don't have is to waste what you do have." The truth is that many are successful because they didn't have the advantages others had. People with enterprise accomplish more than others because they go ahead and do it before they are ready.

Epicurus said, "Do not spoil what you have by desiring what you have not; but remember that what you now have was once among the things you only hoped for." Henri-Frédéric Amiel observed, "Almost everything comes from almost nothing."

No improvement is as certain as that which proceeds from the right and timely use of what you already have. Mike Murdock said, "Whatever God has already given to you will create anything else He has promised to you." Everyone who has arrived had to begin where they were.

The truth is, you can't know what you can do until you try. The most important thing about reaching your dream is starting right where you are. Edward Hale said, "I cannot do everything, but still I can do something; and because I cannot do everything, I will not refuse to do the something that I can do."

The only place to start is where you are.

124

What's one regret you don't want to have?

A safe place is not an easy place to leave. There will be people who won't associate with you anymore, and there will be a recording in your head replaying all the stories you've heard of those who ventured out and failed. But leaving your comfort zone, when it's right, will be absolutely life changing. You'll discover there's a great big world out there waiting to be impacted by your gifts. Years from now, you'll wonder why you didn't leave earlier.

As you look back on your career and life to date, where do you wish you'd been more courageous, believed in yourself more, and been less hesitant in the steps you took?

Anything come to mind? When I talk with friends in their forties and beyond, many tell me that if they could do their life over again, they'd have taken more risks, gone that extra mile, not quit so quickly, settled only for excellence, and spoken up more often. In short, they wished they'd been more dauntless in the risks they'd taken. Henry Van Dyke said, "Time is too slow for those who wait, too swift for those who fear, too long for those who grieve, too short for those who rejoice, but for those who love, time is eternity."

According to Herbert Casson, "'Safety first' has been the motto of the human race . . . but it has never been the motto of leaders. A leader must face danger. He must take the risk and the blame and the brunt of the storm." If you want to be successful, you must either have a chance or take one. You can't get your head above water if you never stick your neck out.

The Bible says there is a season to everything (Eccles. 3:1). Everything. The key is to do what *God* says—*no one* else. Take whatever action you believe you should with integrity. To stay when you're supposed to leave is wrong. To not take the steps shown to you is wrong. Every time.

A dream that does not include risk is not worthy of being called a dream. Edward Halifax said, "The man who leaves nothing to chance will do few things badly, but he will do very few things." If you never take risks, you'll never accomplish great things. Everyone dies, but not everyone has lived.

C. S. Lewis said, "The safest road to hell is a gradual one—the gentle slope, soft underfoot, without sudden turnings, without milestones, without signposts." Elizabeth Kenny reflected, "It is better to be a lion for a day than a sheep all your life." If you dare for nothing, you need hope for nothing.

If you don't risk anything, you risk even more. John Newman wrote, "Calculation never made a hero." All people have a chance to improve themselves, but some just don't believe in taking chances. I agree with Lois Platford when she said, "You have all eternity to be cautious in when you're dead." Being destined for greatness requires you to take risks and confront great hazards.

You'll always miss 100 percent of the shots that you don't take. I agree with John Stemmons when he said, "When your chances are slim and none . . . go with slim." Morris West said, "If you spend your whole life waiting for the storm, you'll never enjoy the sunshine." No one reaches the top without daring.

Be bold and don't settle for only what others give you. Resist the temptation to stay in a rut rather than find your own destiny. Chuck Yeager remarked, "You don't concentrate on risk. You concentrate on results. No risk is too great to prevent the necessary job from getting done."

Whenever you see a successful person, I guarantee that person took risks and made courageous decisions. Success favors the bold. The world is a book where those who do not take risks read only one page. David Mahoney said, "Refuse to join the cautious crowd that plays not to lose. Play to win."

Metastasio observed, "Every noble acquisition is attended with its risks; he who fears to encounter the one must not expect to obtain the other." Listen to Tommy Barnett: "Many people believe that you are really walking by faith when there is no risk, but the truth is the longer you walk with God . . . the greater the risk." If you have found yourself throughout life never scared, embarrassed, disappointed, or hurt, it means you have never taken any chances.

David Viscott wrote, "If your life is ever going to get better, you'll have to take risks. There is simply no way you can grow without taking chances." You have a chance to improve yourself. Just believe in taking chances.

Safety last!

Question 34

What would your life look like if you were the most grateful, thankful person you know?

In 2003, I noticed a shortness of breath when I would cut the yard, pull the trash can up the hill to our street, and walk up hills on the golf course. I decided to go to my doctor and have him check me out. I thought maybe I was having some allergy problems or something like that.

It didn't take him long, after talking with me and doing some tests, to quickly set up some additional steps to get to the bottom of this issue. Within a few days, I found out I had five blocked arteries. Some were blocked nearly 100 percent.

Of course, this was a shock to my wife and me, and we dealt with a fair amount of fear about it. But much greater than our concerns was an overwhelming feeling of thankfulness. God had allowed me to have symptoms and go to a good doctor, and He provided a way for me to correct my situation.

I saw I had much more to be grateful for than anything to be afraid of.

I'm not saying that the process was easy. It wasn't. Opening your chest and having eighty-five staples in your body is not a picnic. But I was offered a choice. Could I see the good in this? I chose to be grateful, and what a difference it made. I was supernaturally peaceful and thankful going into that surgery.

That decision still influences and impacts me today. I am thankful to God.

God gives each of us the gift of 1,440 minutes each day. Have you used one to say thank you? As someone once said, "It's a poor frog who doesn't praise his own pond."

If the only prayer you say in your whole life is "Thank You," I think that would probably be enough. Do you have an attitude of gratitude? If we stop to think more, we would stop to thank more. Of all the human feelings, gratitude has the shortest memory.

Cicero said, "A thankful heart is not only the greatest virtue, but the parent of all other virtues." The degree that you are thankful is a sure index of your spiritual health. Max Lucado wrote, "The devil doesn't have to steal anything from you, all he has to do is make you take it for granted." Replace regret with gratitude. Be grateful for what you have, not regretful for what you have not. If you can't be thankful for what you have, be thankful for what you have escaped. Henry Ward Beecher said, "The unthankful heart . . . discovers no mercies; but the thankful heart . . . will find in every hour, some heavenly blessings." The more you complain, the less you'll obtain.

"If we get everything that we want, we will soon want nothing that we get," Vernon Luchies observed. Francis Schaeffer said, "The beginning of men's rebellion against God was, and is, the lack of a thankful heart." The seeds of discouragement will not grow in a thankful heart. Erich Fromm remarked, "Greed is a bottomless pit which exhausts the person in an endless effort to satisfy the need without ever reaching satisfaction."

Epicurus reflected, "Nothing is enough for the man to whom enough is too little." It's a sure sign of mediocrity to be moderate with our thanks. Don't find yourself so busy asking God for favors that you have no time to thank Him. I relate to what Joel Budd said: "I feel like I'm the one who wrote 'Amazing Grace.'"

"Happiness always looks small while you hold it in your hands, but let it go, and you learn at once how big and precious it is," Maxim Gorky commented. I believe we should have the attitude of George Herbert, who said, "Thou that hast given so much to me, give one thing more, a grateful heart." The Bible says in Psalm 95:2, "Let us come before His presence with thanksgiving" (NASB). Our thanks to God should always precede our requests of Him. The Bible challenges us, "In everything give thanks" (1 Thess. 5:18 NASB).

The fact is, we typically offer too few prayers of thanksgiving and of praise. Don't find yourself at the end of your life saying, "What a wonderful life I've had! I only wish I'd appreciated and realized it sooner."

Go from complaining to appreciating.

From hating to loving.

From grumpy to grateful.

From criticizing to complimenting.
From finding fault to finding good.
From thankless to thankful.

> **Do you count your blessings or think
> your blessings don't count?**

Question 35

Are your eyes looking forward?

Looking backward can get you in trouble.

A woman invited some people over for dinner. At the table, she turned to her six-year-old daughter and said, "Would you like to say the blessing?"

The girl replied, "I wouldn't know what to say."

"Just say what you heard Mommy say," her mother answered.

The daughter bowed her head and said, "Lord, why on earth did I invite all these people to dinner?"

If you look back too much, you'll soon be heading that way. Mike Murdock said, "Stop looking at where you've been and start looking at where you can be." Your destiny in life is always forward, never backward. Katherine Mansfield advised, "Make it a rule of life never to regret and never to look back. Regret is an appalling waste of energy. You can't build on it. It's only good for wallowing in."

Consider the words of the apostle Paul: "Forgetting those things which are behind, and reaching forward to those things which are before, I press towards the mark for the prize of the high call of God in Christ Jesus" (Phil. 3:13–14 WBT). You are more likely to make mistakes when you act only on past experiences. Rosy thoughts about the future can't exist when your mind is full of the blues about the past.

A farmer once said his mule was awfully backward about going forward—this is also true of many people today. Are you backward about going forward? Philip Raskin said, "The man who wastes today lamenting yesterday will waste tomorrow lamenting today." Squash the "good old days" bug.

The past is always going to be the way it was. Stop trying to change it. Your future contains more happiness than any past you can remember. Believe that the best is yet to come.

Oscar Wilde said, "No man is rich enough to buy back his past." Consider what W. R. Inge said: "Events in the past may be roughly divided into those which probably never happened and those which do not matter." The more you look back, the less you will get ahead. Thomas Jefferson was right when he said, "I like the dreams of the future better than the history of the past." Many a has-been lives on the reputation of his reputation.

Hubert Humphrey mused, "The good old days were never that good, believe me. The good new days are today, and better days are coming tomorrow. Our greatest songs are still unsung." When feeling disheartened, you will find that it is because you are living in the past. What's a sure sign of stagnation in your life? When you dwell on the past at the expense of the future, you stop growing and start dying.

I agree with Laura Palmer's advice: "Don't waste today regretting yesterday instead of making a memory for tomorrow."

David McNally said, "Your past cannot be changed, but you can change your tomorrow by your actions today." Never let yesterday use up too much of today. It's true what Satchel Paige said: "Don't look back. Something may be gaining on you."

Edna Ferber commented, "Living in the past is a dull and lonely business; looking back strains the neck muscles, causing you to bump into people not going your way." The first rule for happiness is to avoid lengthy thinking on the past. Nothing is as far away as one hour ago. Charles Kettering added, "You can't have a better tomorrow if you are thinking about yesterday all the time." Your past doesn't equal your future.

There is no future in the past.

Question 36

Do you like the sound of your own voice? How does it sound when you're complaining?

If you aren't grateful for what you have now, how could you be happier with more?

Joe was in trouble. . . . He'd forgotten his wedding anniversary.

His wife was mad. She told him, "Tomorrow morning, I expect to find a gift in the driveway that goes from zero to two hundred in six seconds. *And it better be there!!*"

The next morning, Joe got up early and left for work. When his wife woke up, she looked out the window, and sure enough there was a box gift-wrapped in the middle of the driveway. Confused, she put on her robe, ran out to the driveway, and brought the box back inside the house.

She opened it and found . . . a brand-new bathroom scale.

Joe's been missing since Friday.

If you aren't grateful for what you have, you may not really want more.

Recently I saw a sign under a mounted largemouth bass. It read, "If I had kept my mouth shut I wouldn't be here." How true! What we say is important. The book of Job reminds us, "How forcible are right words!" (6:25). Let me pose this question for you: What would happen if you made your biggest problem your biggest opportunity?

Our prayer to God ought to be, "Oh Lord, please fill my mouth with worthwhile stuff, and nudge me when I've said enough." Proverbs 29:11 says, "A fool uttereth all his mind." Always speak less than you know. Never let your tongue say what your head must pay for later. The human tongue is only a few inches from the brain, but when you listen to some people talk, they seem miles apart. The tongue runs fastest when the brain is in neutral.

A high school track coach was having difficulty motivating his team to perform at its best. The team developed the distinct reputation of coming in last at every track meet they entered. One factor contributing to this less-than-successful program was the coach's pep talk tactics. His most effective inspiring tool, he thought, was to tell his team, "Keep turning left and hurry back." Your words have the power to start fires or quench passion.

Choose to speak positive, motivating, nice words. Blaise Pascal commented, "Kind words do not cost much. Yet they accomplish much." They make other people good-natured. Sir Wilfred Grenfell said, "Start some kind word on its travels. There is no telling where the good it may do will stop."

Sometimes your biggest enemies and most trustworthy friends are the words you say to yourself. "The words 'I am' are potent words; be careful what you hitch them to. The thing you're claiming has a way of reaching back and claiming you," A. L. Kitselman said. Henry Ward Beecher reflected, "A helping word to one in trouble is often like the switch on a railroad track . . . an inch between a wreck and smooth-rolling prosperity." Johann Lavater said, "Never tell evil of a man, if you do not know it for certainty, and if you know it for a certainty, then ask yourself, 'Why should I tell it?'"

There is life and death in the power of the tongue (see Prov. 18:21). What words have the most powerful effect on you?

Don't jump into trouble mouth first.

Question 37

What have you stopped doing that you need to start doing again?

President Ronald Reagan told this story. A young professional baseball player was at home with a friend and they were talking sports while his wife was in the kitchen preparing lunch. Suddenly their baby began to cry.

Over her shoulder the busy wife said, "Change the baby."

Well, he was a young fellow and embarrassed in front of his friend, so he responded, "What do you mean, 'change the baby'? I'm a professional ballplayer and that's not my line of work."

The wife turned around, put her hands on her hips, and gave him a look that could kill. She said, "Look, buster, you lay the diaper out like a diamond, you put second base on home plate, you put the baby's bottom on the pitcher's mound, you hook up first and third, slide home underneath, and if it starts to rain, the game isn't called. . . . You have to start all over again."

Clint Brown said, "The world will always give you the opportunity to quit, but only the world would call quitting an opportunity." In trying times, too many people quit trying. One of the most powerful success principles ever preached is: *Never give up!*

As an author, I have the privilege of signing many books. I like to write encouraging expressions in each book before I sign my name. One of my most common encouragements is: *Never give up!* Joel Budd remarked, "It isn't the final say so, unless *you* say so."

Nobody and nothing can keep you down unless you decide not to rise again. H. E. Jansen said, "The man who wins may have been counted out several times, but he didn't hear the referee." Find a way *to*, not a way *not to*. A lazy man is always judged by what he doesn't do. The choice of giving up or going on is a defining moment in your life. You cannot turn back the clock. But you can wind it up again.

I have the privilege of knowing Peter Lowe, the founder of the Success Seminars. As we talked, he commented, "The most common trait I have found in all people that are successful is that they have conquered the temptation to give up." One of the best ways to give your best a chance is to rise when you're knocked down.

Too many people stop faster than they start. Instead, follow this English proverb: "Don't fall before you are pushed." Margaret Thatcher understood the principle of not quitting when she advised, "You may have to fight a battle more than once to win it." David Zucker added, "Quit now, you'll never make it. If you disregard this advice, you'll be halfway there."

"I can't!" is the conclusion of fools. Listen to Clare Boothe Luce: "There are no hopeless situations; there are only men who have grown hopeless about them." Admiral Chester Nimitz remarked, "God grant me the courage not to give up what I think is right even though I think it is hopeless." Giving up is the ultimate tragedy. The famous boxer Archie Moore reflected, "If I don't get off the mat, I'll lose the fight."

The choice is simple. You can either stand up and be counted or lie down and be counted out. Defeat never comes to people until they admit it. Your success will be measured by your willingness to keep on trying.

Have the courage to live. Anyone can quit.

When someone asks, "What's new?" what's your answer?

When God stretches you, you never come back to your original shape. God has done that in my life many times.

I've had the opportunity to speak for a wonderful organization in South Africa on a couple of occasions. The second opportunity I was given, my host invited not only me but my entire family. When I finished speaking for him, he generously planned and paid for our whole family to spend a week on a houseboat in Zimbabwe on Lake Kariba.

This all sounded good, but we were about to experience an adventure of a lifetime. Let me begin by saying that we're not outdoorsy-type people. We don't camp; we don't hike; we pretty much prefer hotels, beaches, and room service.

Nevertheless, we flew out of Johannesburg, South Africa, to Harare, Zimbabwe. The first thing we saw after our plane landed were signs everywhere that said, "Malaria Alert." We had all had malaria shots prior to leaving, but this still made us uncomfortable. We were greeted at the airport by the captain and cook, who were going to be with us the whole week on the boat. We loaded into a vehicle with them and soon found ourselves on a houseboat at the edge of the massive lake.

We were about to spend seven days in the middle of nowhere, with two people we'd never met, in a country that was beginning to have some very serious turmoil.

Greeted by malaria nets over every bed and a constant smell of gasoline, we took off in our houseboat. Our week was highlighted by excursions on a small pontoon boat out among the hippos and crocodiles. At that time, we didn't realize how very dangerous this was. (We found out later from the World Health Organization that more than 2,900 people are killed by hippos each year in Africa. One hundred people are killed by lions and around five hundred by crocodiles.) Meals were prepared every day, but they became less appetizing when we found out all the dishes were being washed in the lake.

There were some good times too. The shooting stars at night were amazing. The roars of lions and the sightings of hundreds of elephants, wildebeests, and water buffalo were unforgettable and fascinating. But after seven days of this, we were ready to get back to a more civilized way of living.

Our very last day, we stopped on an island as we were heading back to shore. The island was inhabited by numerous monkeys and baboons that seemed to know exactly what to do when a human's boat showed up in their territory. Within minutes, we were swarmed by several baboons running throughout the whole boat, grabbing every kind of food they could, and running up the hill back to their home. A very fitting end to our wild week.

We left that boat changed, in some ways for the better. We certainly were stretched out of our comfort zone and still talk about that crazy week to this day.

Every time God takes you out of your comfort zone into somewhere new, it may be difficult, but something happens that otherwise would not have. This trip bonded our family in unusual and lasting ways. It's always guaranteed to bring laughter and a series of stories from us.

God's best for you will always take you out of your comfort zone. Don't think that staying where you are, doing what you've always done, with the same people at the same time and the same place, will cause dramatic differences in your life.

Do you know people who are literally at the same place today as they were five years ago? They still have the same dreams, the same problems, the same excuses, the same opportunities, and the same way of thinking. They are standing still in life.

Many people basically unplug their clocks at a certain point in time and stay at that fixed moment the rest of their lives. But God's will for us is to grow, to continue to learn and improve. The biggest room in our house is always the room for self-improvement.

Remember this famous saying: "It's what you learn after you know it all that counts." I must admit that I am somewhat of a fanatic about this. I hate to have idle time—time in which I am not learning anything. Those around me know that I must always have something to read or to write during any idle moment that might arise. In fact, I try to learn from everyone. From one I may learn what *not* to do, while from another I learn what *to* do. Learn from the mistakes of others. You can never live long enough to make all the mistakes yourself. You can learn more from a wise man who is wrong than a fool who is right.

Goethe said, "Everybody wants to be somebody; nobody wants to grow." I agree with Van Crouch: "You will never change your actions until you change your mind." An important way to keep growing is to never stop asking questions. The person who is afraid of asking is ashamed of learning. Only hungry minds can grow.

We should all know what we are running from and to, and why. We should learn as if we will live forever and live as if we are going to die tomorrow. Henry Ford said, "Anyone who stops learning is old, whether at twenty or eighty. Anyone who keeps on learning not only remains young, but becomes consistently more valuable regardless of physical capacity." The apostle Paul instructs Timothy, "Study to shew thyself approved unto God" (2 Tim. 2:15). It's fun to keep learning. Learning brings new, interesting people you now have a common understanding with into your life.

Learn from others. Learn to see in the challenges of others the ills you should avoid. Experience is a present possession that keeps us from repeating the past in the future. Life teaches us by giving us new problems before we solve the old ones. Think education is costly or difficult? Listen to Derek Bok: "If you think education is expensive—try ignorance."

Today a reader, tomorrow a leader. (W. Fusselman)

When was the last time you said, "Wow, I can't believe I did that"?

A game warden noticed how a fellow named Sam consistently caught more fish than anyone else. Whereas the other guys would only catch three or four a day, Sam would come in off the lake with a full boat. Stringer after stringer was always packed with freshly caught trout. The warden, curious, asked Sam his secret. The successful fisherman invited the game warden to accompany him and observe.

The next morning the two met at the dock and took off in Sam's boat. When they got to the middle of the lake, Sam stopped the boat, and the warden sat back to see how it was done.

Sam's approach was simple. He took out a stick of dynamite, lit it, and threw it in the air. The explosion rocked the lake with such force that dead fish immediately began to surface. Sam took out a net and started scooping them up.

Well, you can imagine the reaction of the game warden. When he recovered from the shock of it all, he began yelling at Sam. "You can't do this! I'll put you in jail, buddy! You will be paying every fine there is in the book!"

Sam, meanwhile, set his net down and took out another stick of dynamite. He lit it and tossed it in the lap of the game warden with these words: "Are you going to sit there all day complaining, or are you going to fish?"

The poor warden was left with a fast decision to make. He was yanked in one second from an observer to a participant. A dynamite of a choice had to be made, and quickly!

Life is like that. Few days go by without our coming face-to-face with uninvited, unanticipated, yet unavoidable opportunities and decisions.

Always pick an obstacle big enough to matter when you overcome it. Until you give yourself to some great cause, you haven't begun to fully live. Nothing significant is ever accomplished by a realistic person. One of the greatest pleasures you can find is doing what people say you cannot do.

Tradition offers no hope for the present and makes no preparation for the future. Day by day, year by year, broaden your horizon. Russell Davenport remarked, "Progress in every age results only from the fact that there are some men and women who refuse to believe that what they knew to be right cannot be done."

Know the rules and then break some. Melvin Evans said, "The men who build the future are those who know that greater things are yet to come, and that they themselves will help bring them about. Their minds are illumined by the blazing sun of hope. They never stop to doubt. They haven't time."

Be involved in something bigger than you. God has never had anyone qualified working for Him yet. "We are the wire; God is the current. Our only power is to let the current pass through us," Carlo Carretto observed. Be a mind through which Christ thinks, a heart through which Christ loves, a voice through which Christ speaks, and a hand with which Christ helps.

If you want to defend what you believe, live it. Dorothea Brande stated, "All that is necessary to break the spell of inertia and frustration is this: act as if it were impossible to fail." Do an about-face that turns you from failure to success. Keep this advice in mind: always act as if it's impossible to fail.

Do what people say cannot be done.

Question 40

What are you amazingly good at?

A pastor stood before his congregation and said, "I have bad news, I have good news, and I have more bad news. The bad news is: the church needs a new roof."

The congregation groaned.

"The good news is: we have enough money for the new roof!"

A sigh of relief rippled through the gathered group.

Then the pastor said, "The bad news is: it's still in your pockets."

The good news is that God has equipped you with everything you need to fulfill His plans for you. Don't leave it "in your pockets." Do something with the gifts, talents, and strengths He's given you.

Many people devote their whole lives to fields of endeavor that have nothing to do with the gifts God has given them. Incredibly, many spend their entire lives trying to change the way God made them.

God knew what He was doing when He put specific gifts, talents, and strengths inside of you. The book of 1 Corinthians asserts, "Each one has his own gift from God" (7:7 NKJV). Marcus Aurelius said, "Take full account of the excellencies which you possess, and in gratitude remember how you would hanker after them, if you had them not."

Robert Quillen reflected, "If you count all your assets, you always show a profit." Seize the opportunities to use your gifts. "Put yourself on view. This always brings your talents to light," Baltasar Gracián said. Never judge yourself by your weaknesses. I agree with Malcolm Forbes, who claimed, "Too many people overvalue what they are not and undervalue what they are." You are richer than you think you are.

Nathanael Emmons said, "One principal reason why men are so often useless is that they neglect their own profession or calling, and divide and shift their attention among a multitude of objects and pursuits." The best will always arise within you when you tap into the best gifts God put in you. I agree with William Matthews when he said, "One well-cultivated talent, deepened and enlarged, is worth one hundred shallow faculties."

Too many people take only their wants into consideration, never their talents and abilities. Deep down inside, if you are a musician, then make music. If you are a teacher, teach. Be what you are and you will be at peace with yourself. I agree with William Boetcker, who declared, "The more you learn what to do with yourself, and the more you do for others, the more you will learn to enjoy the abundant life." Do what's most natural for you. A Yoruban proverb says, "You can't stop a pig from wallowing in the mud."

I agree with Sydney Harris: "Ninety percent of the world's woe comes from people not knowing themselves, their abilities, their frailties, and even their real virtues." Don't expect anything original from an echo. Alfred de Musset said, "How glorious it is and how painful—to be an exception." Billy Wilder added, "Trust your own instinct. Your mistakes might as well be your own, instead of someone else's." Abraham Lincoln mused, "Whatever you are, be a good one."

E. E. Cummings advised, "To be nobody but yourself—in a world which is doing its best, night and day, to make you everybody else—means to fight the hardest battle which any human being can fight, and never stop fighting."

The bottom line is: be yourself!

Be what you are.

A Final Word

Life's most important answers are found in asking the right questions. I believe every answer you seek is there for you, waiting to be unlocked by the right questions.

Apply these questions and watch your life expand upward. Share them with those you have relationships with and watch their lives improve.

Finally, as you ask yourself the life-changing questions within these pages, be sure to do something with the answers.

John Mason is an internationally recognized bestselling author, speaker, minister, and author coach. He's the founder and president of Insight International and Insight Publishing Group.

He has authored twenty-five books, including *An Enemy Called Average*, *You're Born an Original—Don't Die a Copy*, *Let Go of Whatever Holds You Back*, and *Know Your Limits—Then Ignore Them*, which have sold over two million copies and have been translated into thirty-eight languages throughout the world. His books are widely known as a source of godly wisdom, scriptural motivation, and practical principles. Seven of his books have reached the number one spot on an Amazon bestseller list. His writings have twice been published in *Reader's Digest*, along with numerous other national and international publications.

Known for his quick wit, powerful thoughts, and insightful ideas, John is a popular speaker across the United States and around the world. He and his wife, Linda, have four children and three adorable grandchildren.

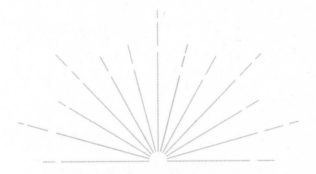

Find More Wisdom from

John Mason

freshword.com |

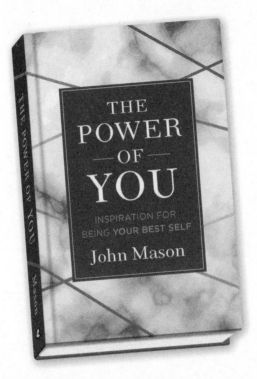